Let's make a patchwork quilt

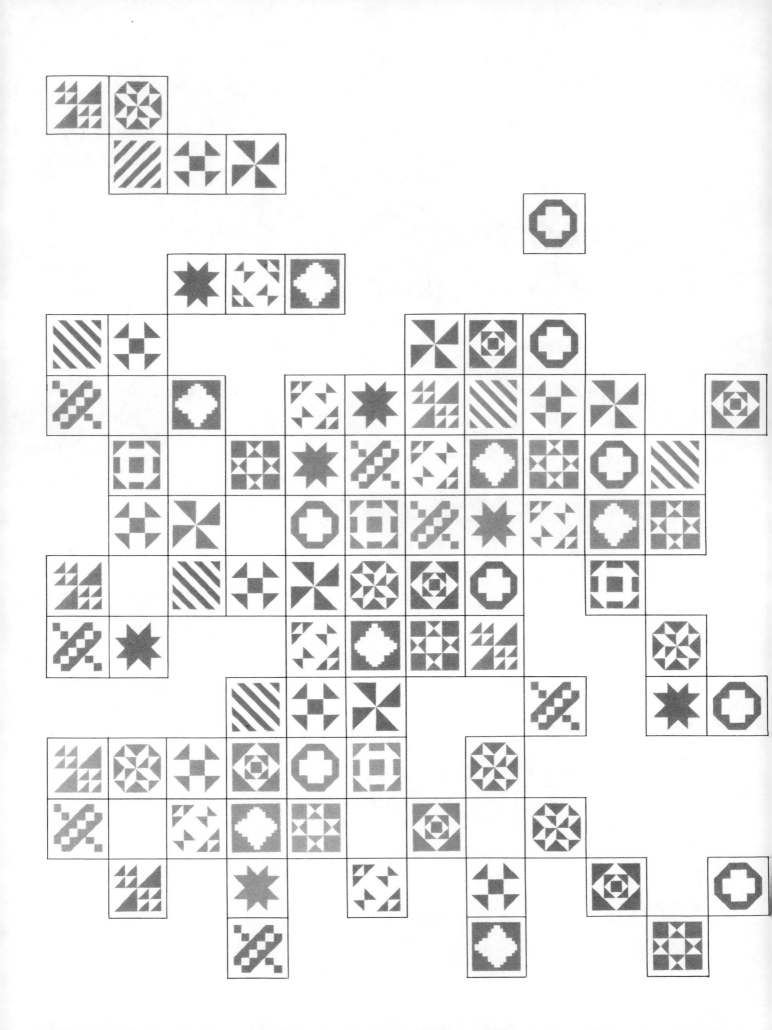

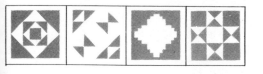

Let's make a patchwork quilt
–using a variety of sampler blocks

JESSIE MacDONALD and MARIAN H. SHAFER

Book Design: Michael P. Durning

Photos: Fred Carbone;
except pages 8 (Fig. 1) and plate 4,
by Michael P. Durning

Illustrations: Len Epstein

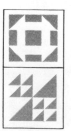

FARM JOURNAL, INC.
Philadelphia, Pennsylvania

Distributed to the trade by
Doubleday & Company, Inc.
Garden City, New York

We dedicate this book to all who dream of making their own first quilts.

Acknowledgements: We are grateful to Patricia J. Morris who introduced us to each other and who has faithfully kept us abreast of what's happening in quilting.

We appreciate the help and interest of Eva Chambers, Helen Collins, Jane Hulse, Jane MacDonald, Carol Mankin and June Read who read our earliest manuscript and made useful as well as encouraging comments about our book.

And most of all, we thank Jean Gillies who took us by the hands and led us to the accomplishment of our dreams— *Let's Make a Patchwork Quilt.*

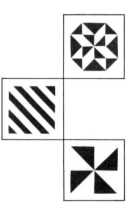

Contents:

Part One

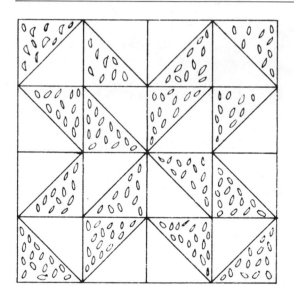

A beginner's guide

For the past few years, we have been teaching the art of making patchwork quilts—with happy results. We know our methods work because they produce both quilts and enthusiastic quilters.

In this section, we guide you, step by step, in making 25 different quilt block designs. Then we help you put some of the blocks (they're all 15" square when finished) into a Beginner's Sampler Quilt, just as we do in our classes.

You begin with simple patterns so you can concentrate on learning the basic techniques. Patterns are arranged in a special order, with each design group chosen to help you master certain skills. After you complete a few patterns, we show you how to turn one block into a miniature quilt—a pillow. This in-troduces you to the quilting stitch and gives you the "feel" of actual quilting.

So, please go through the book page by page from the beginning. Don't skip sections or you may miss something helpful. If you are a beginner, we urge you to work your way through Part One. If you are an experienced quilter, we suggest you read Part One to check our basic methods, with the hope that you will find some useful hints along the way.

Welcome to the fascinating world of quilting!

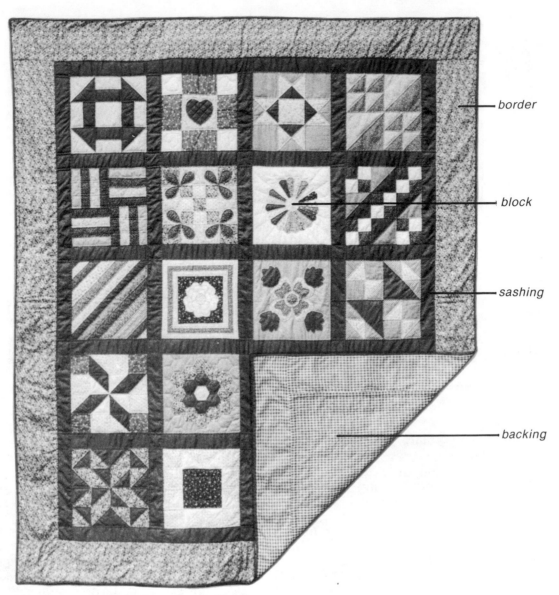

border

block

sashing

backing

Fig. 1 Beginner's Sampler Quilt

Fig. 2 Pieced work block

Fig. 3 Appliqué block

1 Learn the basics – meanings and materials

Work along with us and we'll show you how to make a quilt similiar to the one pictured on the opposite page in Fig. 1. It's our Beginner's Sampler Quilt, shown in a size to fit a full (double) bed. Each block is a different design, but all the colors and prints are coordinated so they can be used together.

A quilter's vocabulary

To help you understand the language of quilting, we'll explain the various terms, using the Beginner's Sampler Quilt for reference.

The quilt is composed of squares or *blocks.* The blocks are framed with strips of fabric called *sashing* or *lattice,* which is used to assemble or *set* the blocks together. The sashed blocks are surrounded by another frame or *border* of printed fabric, and the finished unit is called a *quilt top.*

The quilt itself is like a sandwich, with three layers. The quilt top goes over *batting,* a nonwoven middle layer that gives the quilt thickness. The bottom layer is the *backing,* and usually is made with lengths of fabric sewed together to form one big sheet the size of the quilt top. The three layers are held together with small *quilting stitches.*

We use the term *patchwork* to describe all the quilt blocks you'll find in this book. Some are *pieced work,* made by sewing (or piecing) together small shapes of fabric to form one large block. These designs usually have geometric shapes, such as squares and triangles, as in Fig. 2, although some advanced designs use curves.

Other patchwork blocks are made with *appliqué,* a technique of layering one or more pieces of fabric on top of a large square of another fabric, then sewing in place. Appliqué designs often have free-form shapes, as in Fig. 3.

You will find exact size patterns for all designs in this book, except for a few squares and rectangles too large to fit on a page. These patterns should be copied and cut from a sturdy material to make *templates,* which will be used to trace the patterns onto fabric. You can use cardboard, posterboard or plastic. We've found that large plastic coffee-can lids make excellent templates.

You may trace patterns directly from the book, or you may draft the patterns, using the dimensions given. You will have to measure and draw those few large squares and rectangles we mentioned, but we suggest that you also try

drafting some triangles and other shapes, too—just to learn the technique. Then you will be able to copy other patterns in the future, and you'll also be able to create your own patchwork designs.

Whatever method you use, try to be accurate. An excellent way to check your work is to place your template over our pattern in the book. If there is a discrepancy, go back to the drawing board. Try again.

To use the template, place it on the fabric and trace around it with a pencil. This line is the *sewing line.* When you cut the fabric, you must allow approximately ½″ beyond the pencil line for a seam allowance; this is the *cutting line.* You can measure and draw the seam allowance, or you can gauge it by eye. (The seam allowance will later be trimmed, so it can vary a bit.) We prefer to mark only the sewing line, then use our eyes to judge the cutting line. With practice, it's easy to do.

Straight grain and bias

Throughout the book you will be given reminders to cut fabric on the straight of fabric or *straight grain.* "What," you may ask, "is straight grain?" This applies to woven fabrics, and Fig. 4 should clear up the mystery. You probably know

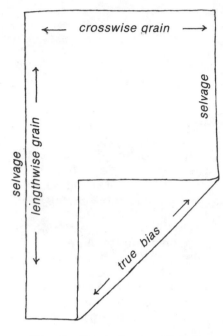

Fig. 4 Grain lines of fabric

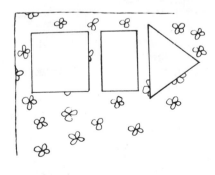

Fig. 5 Placing templates on fabric

the selvage is the woven edge of the fabric. The lengthwise grain (or lengthwise thread) runs parallel to it and has very little stretch. The crosswise grain (or crosswise thread) runs from selvage to selvage and may have a little stretch For patchwork, we use both lengthwise and crosswise grains as straight grain or straight of fabric.

Now, consider *bias.* If you turn up one corner of the fabric (Fig. 4) so that the crosswise grain is parallel to the lengthwise grain, you form a 45° angle. The diagonal line of the fold is the true bias, and it has the most stretch.

You can test this stretch quality quickly by handling woven fabric. First, hold a section of fabric along the straight grain and pull. Not much stretch there. Then hold the fabric on the diagonal and pull. See the difference? The bias really stretches.

So you must be especially careful when you work with bias edges to avoid stretching them. Otherwise, you'll put puckers into your work, and edges that should match won't come out even.

Try to avoid bias edges if possible. When cutting a square or rectangle, place it so that all sides line up with the straight grain (Fig. 5). In the case of a triangle, we suggest you place the longest side of the template on the straight grain.

Choosing fabric

Woven fabric of all cotton is the traditional fabric for quilts, and some people claim it is the easiest to work with. Another choice these days is a woven blend of cotton and polyester. You may end up using a mix of these two, just to get the colors and prints you want.

A quilt made of colorfast, washable fabric such as cotton or cotton-polyester blend and filled with a polyester batting should be completely washable. If you do plan to wash the finished quilt, it is wise to preshrink every piece of fabric before you cut it. Just wash and dry the fabric as you will wash and dry the finished quilt. If you find that a fabric is not colorfast or that it wrinkles too much, put it away for some other use. Don't sew it into your quilt.

If you plan to dry-clean the finished quilt, you needn't preshrink the fabric. In this case, take a small piece of muslin and write on it in indelible ink, "Dry-Clean Only." Sew this patch to the back of the finished quilt.

Mixing colors

Your fabric choice probably will begin with color. This is a very personal thing, and the colors you like to look at and live with will influence the colors you choose for your quilt.

You can mix many different colors, or just a few. Or you can stick with variations of one color. Whatever your choice, try to combine colors with light, medium and dark values. A quilt made of all light or all dark colors tends to be rather dull.

Our Beginner's Sampler Quilt, shown on plate 1, combines beige (light), rust (medium) and brown (dark). An equally attractive color scheme could be monochromatic, using different values of just one color with white.

Browse through this book, and you'll see a variety of color combinations. You may find the color grouping that is just right for you.

For your quilt, we suggest you choose three solid

colors—one light, one medium and one dark. Then, add prints in light, medium and dark values that blend with the solid colors. You could begin with one or two prints, then choose the solids to match. You want prints that go with each other as well as with the solid colors.

As you make each patchwork block, vary the prints and solids in a way that pleases you, but try to follow the principle of using a combination of light, medium and dark values in each block. When just two fabrics are needed for a design, combine two different values.

Plan to repeat all the fabrics that you use. If there is a light print in one pieced block, echo it in another pieced design and again in an appliqué block. Repeating the same print at least two or three times gives continuity to the quilt. Using pieces of the sashing and border fabrics in some of the blocks also increases the continuity.

Take time to choose color and fabric combinations that you really like. Enjoy seeing the varied effects you can achieve by mixing fabrics. You will feel like an artist.

The real fun of fabric selection begins when you search for prints. If you have a scrap bag, look there first. Your quilt will have special meaning if it includes pieces of your daughter's favorite dresses or your son's favorite shirts. If you find scraps compatible with the quilt color scheme, wash and press them and put them aside.

You probably will make several trips to fabric stores before you find all the prints that you want. Buy prints in ¼- or ½-yd. lengths, and try to choose a variety of eight

or 10 different ones.

It will help to cut swatches from all the fabrics that you accumulate and pin or tape them to cardboard, as in Fig. 6. Take this swatch card with you every time you go fabric shopping to help you match colors accurately and to avoid duplicating prints. As you buy new fabrics, add swatches of these to the card.

Write the name of the store where you purchased each fabric beside the swatch on your fabric card. Even though you have ample fabric to complete the quilt, you may find that you want just a little more of one print for a block. The extra fabric you accumulate this way can be used to make matching pillows. Or you can use it in your next quilt. (We must warn you that quiltmaking can be habit forming!)

Try our combinations

To make it easier for you to follow the directions in cutting and assembling the designs in this book, we have listed sample combinations of fabrics to use. For example, we may suggest you choose one solid color and one print that go together. Or we may recommend you select a light solid color and two prints— one light, and one dark.

This is simply a teaching aid. Patchwork blocks can be made with any combination of solid colors and prints, and any combination of light and dark fabrics that you choose. There are no rules. Each quilt pictured in the book reflects the individual quilter's taste and creativity.

Fig. 6   Fabric swatch card

Yardage for beginner's blocks and quilt top				
Type of fabric, 45″ wide	twin	full (double)	queen	king
Solid color for sashing, bias binding and some blocks	3¾ yd.	4¼ yd.	4¼ yd.	4¾ yd.
Print for border, a pillow back and some blocks	3 yd.	3½ yd.	4 yd.	4½ yd.
Solid colors for blocks: First color Second color	½ yd. ½ yd.	½ yd. ½ yd.	½ yd. ½ yd.	1 yd. 1 yd.
Assorted prints for blocks, ¼ to ½ yd. each	3 yd.	3 yd.	3 yd.	4 yd.
Number of blocks needed	15	20	20	25

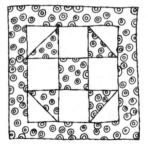

A. Good example

B. Poor example

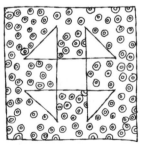

Fig. 7   Use of sashing fabric in a quilt block

How much fabric?

The chart above lists enough yardage so that you can complete all the sampler blocks in Part One and also a Beginner's Sampler Quilt Top. (We'll discuss backing fabric and batting later on when you need them.)

If you do complete all the block designs in Part One — and we hope you do — you will have more blocks than you need for most quilt sizes, though not quite enough for a king. Consider turning left-over blocks into pillows or tote bags. For a king-size quilt, make duplicates of your favorite blocks.

When you have finally assembled all the fabrics, and before you begin making blocks, be sure to cut off and save the yardage needed for sashing, border and binding. Take the sashing fabric (a solid color) and carefully cut ¼ yd. from one end to use in making blocks. Cut off another piece, 1 yd. square, and label it "Binding." Take the remaining length and label it "Sashing."

Then take the border fabric (a print), and cut off ½ yd. from one end. This is to use in making blocks and a pillow cover. Label the remaining length "Border." Put the binding, sashing and border fabrics aside until later.

A few words of caution about using the sashing fabric in block patterns: You want the finished blocks to look framed and separate from the sashing. So avoid using the sashing fabric along the edge of the block. Otherwise, you won't be able to tell where the design ends and the sashing begins. See Fig. 7 and plate 2 for examples.

Other supplies

In addition to fabrics for the quilt top, you will need to collect a variety of sewing supplies and materials to make the Beginner's Sampler Quilt. These include:

• *Template material* of posterboard, cardboard or plastic. Save those large coffee-can lids.

• *Dressmaker's carbon paper* (made especially for use on fabrics) in white and blue.

• *No. 2 (soft) pencil* for tracing around templates on light-colored fabrics.

• *Yellow pencil* for tracing around templates on dark fabrics.

• *No. 5H or 6H (hard) pencil* for transferring quilting designs to fabric. You need a pencil that won't smudge.

• *Black felt-tip pen* with a fine line for drawing quilting designs on templates.

• *Tracing paper* for transferring quilting or embroidery designs to dark fabric.

• *Paper clips* for anchoring

layers of paper when tracing patterns from book.
• *Masking tape* for anchoring fabric to templates.
• *12″ ruler* with a metal edge
• *Yardstick* for measuring border lengths and making large templates.
• *T-square ruler or a triangle* (Fig. 8) for making perfectly square corners.
• *Sharp dressmaker's shears* for cutting fabrics.
• *Old scissors or shears* for cutting templates and paper.
• *Sharp pins.* We prefer ball-point pins because they go into the fabric easily and stay in place.
• *T-pins.* These are helpful when you put a whole quilt top together. Buy them later if you need them.
• *Needles.* Use Sharps for handwork and basting. Use Betweens (size 7 or 8) for quilting. Betweens are short and tough, the kind you need for quilting. Short needles help you make short stitches.

You may also want embroidery needles for fancy stitching with embroidery floss, and a large darning needle for basting large areas.
• *A thimble!* Even if you've never used one before, try it now. It really protects your finger.
• *White thread,* mercerized cotton No. 50, for basting and for stitching by machine or by hand.
• *Colored thread* in mercerized cotton or cotton-wrapped polyester to match appliqué fabrics. You may also want to use colored thread instead of white for stitching fabric pieces together.
• *Embroidery floss* to match or contrast with appliqué fabrics.
• *Quilting thread* to match or contrast with the quilt fabrics. This thread is strong and lustrous and doesn't knot as

easily as other types. It is the best thread to use for quilting. However, if you can't find the color you need, you can use mercerized cotton and wax it with beeswax to add strength and to cut down on knotting and tangling. Polyester thread is not as good for this hand sewing because it tends to knot and stretch. If you must use polyester for color matching, cut it into strands no longer than 18″ and wax it thoroughly.
• *Beeswax,* if you need it for waxing thread. This is sold with sewing supplies.
• *Inexpensive muslin* or other soft cotton. This is used for backing some blocks, and it won't show.
• *Backing fabric* for quilt (this will show) and *bonded polyester batting.* Buy these later when you are ready to put your quilt together.
• *Large round hoop* for quilting (optional, depending on how you do your quilting). Decide on this later.
• Finally, you will need the *desire* to make a Beginner's Sampler Quilt, plus time and patience and an adventure-some spirit!

Are you ready to start?

If you have some sizable scraps of two fabrics that go together, you might want to try the first sampler block in Chapter 3 right away.

Meanwhile, as you shop and assemble materials for your quilt, why not read through Chapter 2? You will find that quilting has a long and fascinating history, and that the quilt you are about to make could become a cherished family heirloom.

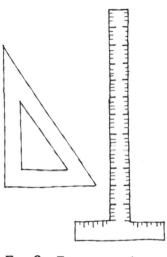

Fig. 8   T-square ruler and triangle

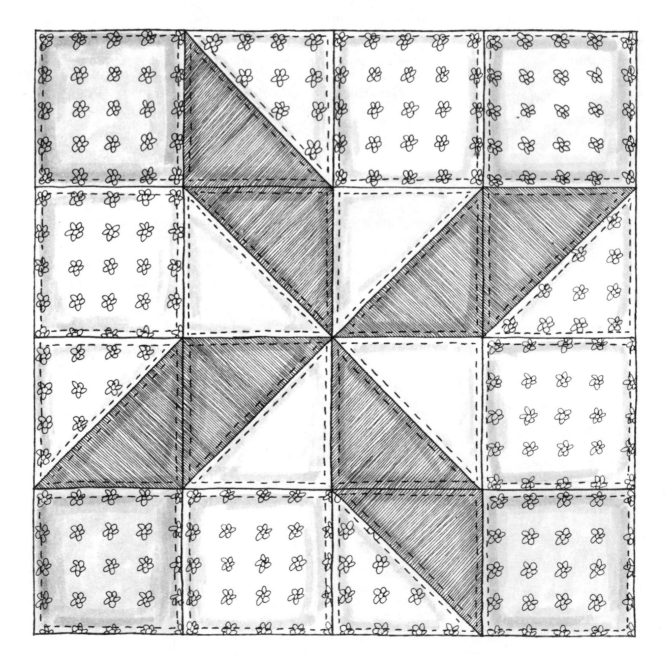

2 Skim a little history of quilts

Quilts were such an important part of early American life that many people think the settlers actually invented them. Colonial women certainly spent a lot of time quilting, and they leaned heavily on true "patch" work, but quilting itself goes back thousands of years. Archeologists have found examples of quilting done as long ago as 5,000 B.C., our earliest recorded history. It's possible that people were quilting even before then.

The British Museum has a statue of Menes, the Egyptian king who lived about 3,400 B.C., which shows him wearing a quilted jacket. Records indicate that quilting was an established art form in Egypt at that time, and that it was often done by men.

When a tomb was unearthed in China in the 1900s, scientists found it belonged to a Mongolian warlord who lived in 1 B.C. Among its treasures was a rug, quilted in a scroll design that is still in use today.

Ancient quilted fabric was often plain, so that any design was formed by the quilting stitches. However, appliqué and pieced work also have a long history, dating to before the time of Christ. For example, the heads of Egyptian mummies often were wrapped in fabric, arranged to form a design we know today as Log Cabin.

The Bible makes references to quilting, and history books tell us that some soldiers wore quilted garments under their armor.

From the East to Europe

Marco Polo probably introduced the first quilts to Europe about 1200. He found them on his famous trip to the Orient and returned home with prized examples. It's believed that many of these quilts had elaborate designs. Later, the Crusaders discovered quilts in the Middle East. These often displayed mosaic designs, and probably were the inspiration for the pattern we know as Grandmother's Flower Garden.

By 1400, quilting was widely practiced throughout Europe and it was as popular in castles as in cottages. Some famous royal quilters included Catherine of Aragon (who invented black embroidery), Catherine de Medici, and Marie Theresa of Austria (Marie Antoinette's mother).

In his will, Shakespeare bequeathed all the quilts and bedclothing of the second-best bedroom in his home to his wife, Anne Hathaway. Many historians believe his wife was an accomplished quilter and probably made the quilts herself.

By the time America was colonized in 1620, European women were thoroughly trained in the art of quilting. Girls learned to sew when they were three or four years old, and a girl often made her first quilt at the age of five. When a young woman was ready for marriage, it was customary for her to have completed 12 quilts, as well as one extra quilt top of intricate design. This last was designated as her marriage quilt and usually was covered with a profusion of appliquéd roses, bells and hearts.

Clay's Choice is a patchwork design named after Henry Clay, U.S. statesman and orator.

Women adapted quilting to their way of life in the early colonies, and they began wearing sewing bags at their waists. In the bags were fabrics for quilt patches, needles, scissors and thread. When a woman had a few minutes to spare, she reached into her bag, selected several pieces of fabric and seamed them together. In time, she had completed a quilt top.

Quilting materials became status symbols. A sewing bag was often decorated with elaborate designs, and the owner liked to be "caught" wearing it so that it could be admired. A homemaker might plan her day so that she patched old, everyday quilts in the mornings. In the afternoons, when visitors called, she could work on her best quilts, which displayed her finest workmanship.

A cultural mix of designs

In addition to the Orient, Middle East and Egypt, other cultures also influenced quilting in the new country. In the South, slaves who quilted for plantation owners and for themselves introduced appliqué symbols representing their native Africa—plants, human figures and the sun. From Native Americans, settlers borrowed the Sawtooth design, which is found in so many popular patterns today. As all these design elements mixed and mingled, "American" quilting emerged.

Quilts in American colonies

Settlers arriving in America in the early 1600s included quilts in their luggage. Even so, the ones who settled in the northern colonies were ill-prepared for the severe winters of the New World. Quilts received heavy use in the drafty cabins and soon needed mending. For this, women cut fabric from worn-out clothing to sew over tears and thin spots. The results were true patch work.

To make new quilts, the settlers eventually turned to homespun fabrics made from home-grown flax and wool. These were stuffed with almost anything on hand, including native grasses, cornhusks, straw, hay, milkweed and even letters from home.

In the late 1600s, Yankee clipper ships were making regular trips from the East Coast, around the Cape of Good Hope to China, and a brisk trade developed. Sailors bought inexpensive cotton throws in the Orient as gifts for their wives and sweethearts, and these fabrics inspired new quilt designs. Sometimes the printed flowers were cut out and appliquéd to homespun fabrics. Other times, the designs were simply copied in quilting stitches, or the fabrics themselves quilted to outline the printed designs.

Gradually, the hit-or-miss patching designs of the early colonial days were replaced with intricate appliqué and pieced work. Patterns were given names such as Pine Tree, Delectable Mountains, Log Cabin, Postage Stamp, Rose of Sharon and Flying Geese. Historical events were commemorated with patterns like 54-40 or Fight, Whig Rose and Clay's Choice. Farm equipment and household

utensils were translated into such patterns as Mill Wheel, Churn Dash and Monkey Wrench.

Quilt patterns were enthusiastically exchanged and became known by different names in different communities. The Bear's Paw design in Kentucky was called Duck's Foot in the Mud in areas where bears were not a threat to life and limb. In Philadelphia Quaker communities, this very same pattern became Hand of Friendship. To add to the confusion, a name might identify a certain design in one community, but quite a different design in another part of the country.

A social activity

Although piecing and appliqué could be done by one person, quilting the finished product was better handled by a group. As a result, our foremothers developed the famous community sewing bees.

Women were not encouraged to congregate in groups, but colonial town fathers would sanction a day for community quilting. On that day, women took their finished quilt tops, along with baskets of food, to the largest home or building in their town. The best quilters were invited to work at the frames, while poor quilters and latecomers were relegated to the kitchen to prepare the food. Late in the day, husbands and children joined the group and a feast was shared by the whole community. Usually seven or eight quilts were completed at the bee.

A popular product of the bee was the freedom quilt, made to celebrate a young man's twenty-first birthday. Until his coming of age, each male was obligated to give all his earnings to his parents, who used the money to help sustain the family. At 21, he was free to control his own earnings. However, this new freedom was often short lived. Many freedom quilts were given directly to the young men's fiancées, who also received bridal quilts. The freedom quilt custom died out in the 1800s, but the quilting bee continues to this day.

Folk art and heirlooms

Over the years, American patchwork has become highly respected throughout the world. It is recognized as true folk art. European museums now have collections of quilts made in this country, and quilting classes taught by American women are popular in the principal cities of Europe.

On this side of the ocean, a tremendous upsurge of interest in quilting began about 1960. Displays, classes and literature about quilting have enjoyed great popularity. As more Americans become aware of this heritage, the value of family quilts is enhanced. (Lucky the families who kept their grandmothers' quilts!)

Department stores, museums, interior decorators and antique dealers have contributed greatly to the popularity of American quilts. With increased interest, prices have gone up. It is not at all unusual for quilt prices to range from $500 to $8,000.

Quilt popularity and high prices have gone overseas, too. Recently, a shop on a quiet street in London was doing a thriving business selling used American quilts of ordinary quality for about $1,000 each.

The value of the quilt you make will far exceed the price tag it could carry, however. It will contain hours of thought, planning and stitching. It may also contain fabrics that have special meaning for you and your family. Perhaps its greatest importance is that it will endure and take its place as an art form as old as history.

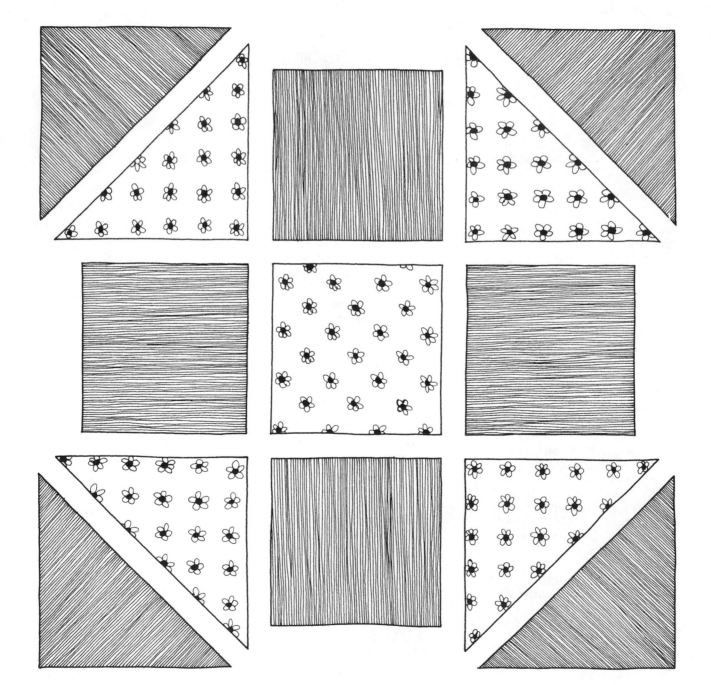

3 Begin with pieced work

Most pieced work designs fit together like puzzles. You cut out various pieces, then sew them together to form one square block. Designs with just a few large pieces are easiest to handle. Pieced work becomes more difficult when designs have more—and smaller—pieces.

NINE-PATCH BLOCKS

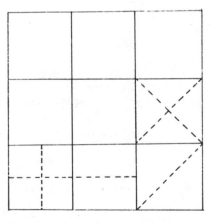

Fig. 9 Basic nine-patch block

For your first blocks, we chose a group of designs called nine-patch. They're easy to do, and you'll understand the name when you look at the square in Fig. 9. The solid lines divide the block into nine smaller squares. Broken lines show how you can divide these small squares to form many different designs.

Hundreds of nine-patch designs already exist. Later, you can experiment with dividing the squares, and you may even create a completely new pattern. But for now, let's concentrate on some traditional nine-patch blocks.

Making the templates

On page 30 are patterns you will use in various combinations to make five different nine-patch blocks. These are based on a 5" square.

The first step is to make templates of all the patterns. One method is to place cardboard, posterboard or sturdy plastic directly under each pattern outline. Slip dressmaker's carbon paper between the page and template material, and secure the layers with paper clips or with pins pushed through the layers. Use a No. 2 pencil (well-sharpened) and a ruler to trace the pattern.

You also can make the templates by taking the measurement of each line, then transferring it to your template material. For this, a T-square ruler or a triangle will help you make perfectly square corners.

After your drawings are complete, label them "Nine-patch A," "Nine-patch B," etc. This will help you quickly identify them later. Then cut out the templates.

Checking for accuracy

For a quick check, place each template on top of our pattern in the book.

Another test is to fit the smaller sections against the larger ones. For example, you have a 5" square A and a 2½" square E. Place the smaller pattern E in one corner of the larger square, exactly on the cutting line, and draw around

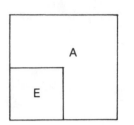

Fig. 10 Checking templates for accuracy

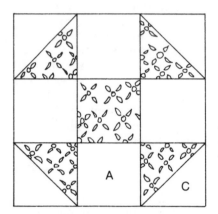

Fig. 11 **Shoofly**
(See also plate 2)

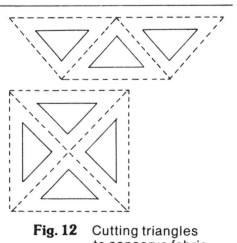

Fig. 12 Cutting triangles to conserve fabric

the small square (Fig. 10). Move E to an adjacent corner and draw around it again. Continue until you have drawn four small squares within the 5" square. If your work is accurate, you will have divided the 5" template into four equal squares.

Note that all remaining pattern pieces (triangles and rectangles) are divisions of the large square A. You can check them all by fitting them into square A or by fitting them into each other. For example, triangle D fits into triangle C, etc.

Templates of posterboard or cardboard wear down with use and become inaccurate. Check them regularly and replace them with new ones when the corners become blunt or the sides get rough.

SHOOFLY

Now, let's make the Shoofly block, shown in Fig. 11. It uses two shapes, square A and triangle C, and it requires two different fabrics. Try a solid color and a print. Read the step-by-step instructions below before cutting:

    A — 4 of solid color
    A — 1 of print
    C — 4 of solid color
    C — 4 of print

Trace and cut

To mark the fabric, lay it face down. Place template A on the *wrong* side of the fabric with the edges on the straight of the fabric (running along the woven threads). Be sure to allow ½" seam allowances all around the template. (You can include the selvage in this if you wish, since it will be trimmed off later.)

Trace around the template with a No. 2 pencil for light

fabric, or a yellow pencil for dark fabric. (Always keep your pencil sharp.) Use template A to mark one print and four solid color pieces.

Cut out the squares, adding ½" seam allowances. You can gauge these by eye or mark them with a pencil if you're uncertain. The pencil lines drawn around the templates are your sewing lines.

Use triangle C to trace four print and four solid color pieces. Place the longest side of the triangle on the straight grain of the fabric, again allowing ½" seam allowances all around. Fig. 12 illustrates two ways to place triangles so that you can use fabric to best advantage; broken lines indicate ½" seam allowances. Trace around the template and cut out the triangles.

Pin-baste

Arrange the cut pieces of fabric in front of you, right side up, following the diagram for Shoofly in Fig. 11. Work with the two triangles in the upper right corner—one print and one solid color. The object is to turn these two triangles into one square.

Begin by pin-basting, and refer to Fig. 13 as you work. Place the triangles, right sides together, and join on the long sides. Place pin 1 where the pencil lines intersect at the right corner. Insert the pin through the top triangle, then slightly separate the two pieces of fabric so that you can guide the pin through the bottom triangle—exactly at the intersection of the corner lines. Anchor pin 1 horizontally through both thicknesses. Make sure it covers the pencil lines on both the top and bottom layers.

Next, insert pin 2 vertically, below the first pin and as

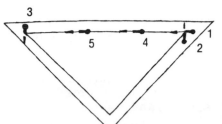

Fig. 13 Pin-basting triangles

Fig. 14 Running stitch

Fig. 15 Single backstitch

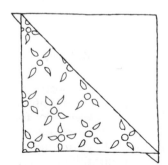

Fig. 16 Joining triangles to form a square

close to it as possible. Bring pin 2 out above pin 1 to anchor it. Insert pin 3 at the left corner of the triangle, making sure it goes through the intersection of the pencil lines on both top and bottom layers. Place this pin vertically through the fabric.

Insert pins 4 and 5 horizontally from right to left, making sure they are exactly on the pencil lines.

Stitch

Now you are ready to sew, either by machine or by hand. Go from raw edge to raw edge, stitching exactly on the drawn pencil lines. Use mercerized cotton or cotton-covered polyester thread.

Machine stitching is faster and produces stronger stitches, and even treasured quilts made as early as 1860 were machine-stitched. Adjust the stitch length for 10 stitches to the inch, and remove all horizontally placed pins (those directly on the seam line) as you come to them. On most machines, you can stitch over the vertically placed pins (those perpendicular to the seam line).

If you choose to do everything by hand, as some traditionalists feel must be done, use the running stitch illustrated in Fig. 14. Begin with a knot at the end of the thread. Weave the point of the needle in and out of the fabric, taking two or more stitches before pulling the needle through. Begin and end each seam with a backstitch (Fig. 15) to make a strong seam. Also make a tiny backstitch at every third or fifth stitch to secure your work. You should aim for at least eight running stitches to the inch.

When you have completed a seam, check to be sure that

you sewed directly over the pencil lines. If any adjustment must be made, now is the time to make it. If the stitching is off just a little, don't worry. If it is off a lot, take it out and do it over.

Open your patch. It will be a square like Fig. 16.

Join the remaining triangles to complete three more squares.

Trim and finger-press

With sharp shears, trim the seam allowances to just under ¼". Do not open the seams, but fold them to one side. If you are using one light and one dark fabric, fold the seam allowances toward the dark fabric (so they won't show through). Finger-press along each seam to smooth it on the right side and to make the seam allowances lie flat on the wrong side. Do this by running the tip of your finger, or fingernail, down the seam. Apply pressure all the way.

Piecing the block

Arrange all nine squares in front of you, right side up, as shown in Fig. 17.

Start at the top with Row 1. Pin each square to the next, right sides together. Use the pin-basting method and carefully match the pencil lines. Then stitch.

Note: When you machine stitch a bias edge (on a triangle) to a straight grain edge (on a square), work with the straight edge on top. Pin along the straight edge, and stitch with the bias side down. The feed dog on the machine helps move the bias fabric along without puckering.

Your top row will look like Fig. 18 when stitched.

Join the squares across Row 2 in the same way. Then complete Row 3.

Place all three rows in front

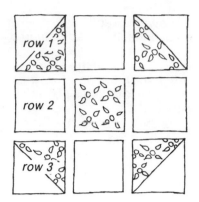

Fig. 17 Pieces for Shoofly block

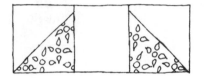

Fig. 18 Top row of Shoofly

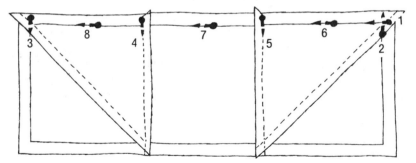

Fig. 19 Pin-basting rows together

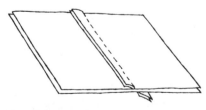

Fig. 20 Alternating directions of seam allowances to distribute bulk

of you again, right side up. This time you will join the rows, right sides together.

Begin at the top, pinning Row 1 to Row 2, as in Fig. 19. Use the same pin-basting sequence, beginning at the right side, with pin 1 horizontal on the sewing lines. Place pin 2 vertically, and as close as possible to pin 1. Place pin 3 vertically at the left side.

It is important to match the stitched seams of the two rows. To do this, place pin 4 vertically, going in where the pencil line intersects the stitched seam on both top and bottom layers. Anchor pin 4 by bringing it back through the stitched seams of both layers. Pin through the seams, not next to them.

Note: When pinning two seams together, try to avoid bunching the seam allowances. For example, turn the

seam allowance on the top layer in one direction, and the seam allowance on the bottom layer in the opposite direction, as in Fig. 20. Try to fold seams under the darkest fabric when you can.

Add pin 5 at the next stitched seam (Fig. 19). Then place additional pins along the seam line to be stitched. Check your work to make sure that your patches are accurately placed and that seam lines match. Stitch, trim the seam allowance, and finger-press your work.

Join Row 3 to Row 2 in the

same manner.

There! You have just completed the Shoofly! Isn't it remarkable how a few strategic stitching lines have completely transformed squares and triangles into a nine-patch block?

Try to remember the steps you followed: trace, cut, pin-baste, stitch, trim, finger-press.

A tradition of "mistakes"

We advocate making the blocks as accurately as possible. However, we think you should know about one of the oldest traditions in needlework.

For at least 5,000 years, it has been the custom of art needleworkers to express their reverence for the gods by making one or more intentional mistakes in their handiwork. They believed that only their God could make a perfect thing. The custom has been noted in Oriental, Mid-Eastern and Native American (notably Navajo) artifacts.

The tradition was faithfully carried out by American quilters. If their quilts were perfectly made, they rectified the situation by painstakingly creating a mistake. Quilt blocks containing errors were called "humility blocks."

If you follow one of the nine-patch designs to its finish and find that one of the pieces has slipped into place—oh, so easily—*backwards*, don't throw the block away or tear it to shreds. Just incorporate your goof into your quilt and call it your humility block.

We should add that true perfection is difficult to achieve. Sometimes a few points won't meet exactly or little puckers appear, even when you have been very careful. These little misses may be quite noticable when

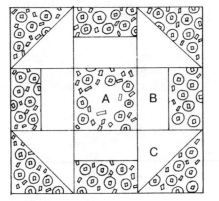

Fig. 21   Churn Dash
(See also plate 2)

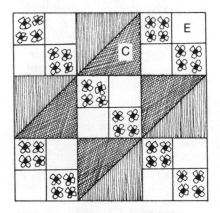

Fig. 22   Greek Cross
(See also plate 2)

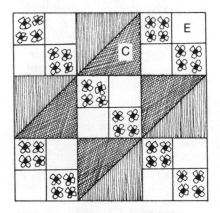

Fig. 23   Jacob's Ladder
(See also plate 3)

the block is flat, but quilting tends to soften the lines and minimize tiny errors. So strive for accuracy, but don't be too hard on yourself.

CHURN DASH

Now that you have successfully completed the Shoofly, let's try the Churn Dash block shown in Fig. 21. This pattern is known by other names, including Monkey Wrench and Hole in the Barn Door. The pattern looks very much like Shoofly, but notice that only one square is undivided. This center square is made of one fabric and the rectangles next to it are in a contrasting fabric to form the design.

For Churn Dash, you will need three templates—square A, rectangle B and triangle C. Use two fabrics—one solid color and one print. On the *wrong* side of the fabric, trace and cut (adding ½″ seam allowances):

    A — 1 of print
    B — 4 of solid color
    B — 4 of print
    C — 4 of solid color
    C — 4 of print

Arrange the pieces in front of you, right side up, using Fig. 21 as a guide. Pin-baste, stitch, trim and finger-press as you did in making the Shoofly block, page 20.

Join the C triangles to make four squares. Join the B rectangles to make four squares. Stitch the squares into rows. Finally, join the rows to complete the block.

GREEK CROSS

Does the pattern in Fig. 22 look familiar? Of course it does. The Greek Cross is

basically the same block as Churn Dash, but the fabrics are arranged differently. Here, the center square and the surrounding rectangles are cut of the same fabric to form the cross. This dramatically illustrates how you can change the appearance of a design.

For the Greek Cross, you need three templates—square A, rectangle B and triangle C. Use two fabrics—both prints, this time. On the *wrong* side of the fabric, trace:

    A — 1 of print No. 1
    B — 4 of print No. 1
    B — 4 of print No. 2
    C — 4 of print No. 1
    C — 4 of print No. 2

Cut out the pieces (adding ½″ seam allowances), and arrange them in front of you with Fig. 22 as your guide.

Join the C triangles to form squares. Pin-baste, stitch, trim and finger-press, using the sequence given for the Shoofly block, page 20.

Join the B rectangles to form squares. Stitch the squares into rows. Finally, join the rows to complete the block.

JACOB'S LADDER

This pattern (Fig. 23) also is a nine-patch, but it looks entirely different from the first three blocks in the chapter. It has more pieces to assemble, but study it carefully and you can see how the design divides into nine basic squares.

The pattern goes back to pre-Revolutionary War days and has a list of other names. It is also known as Tail of Benjamin's Kite, Trail of the Covered Wagon, Underground Railway, and even Road to California.

Jacob's Ladder is a very ef-

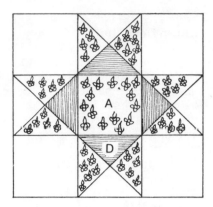

Fig. 24   Ohio Star
(See also plate 3)

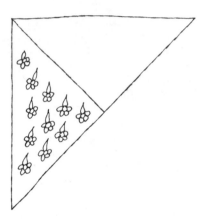

Fig. 25   Joining two small triangles

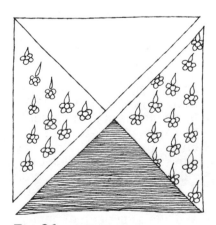

Fig. 26   Joining four triangles to make a square

fective overall pattern that can be arranged in many ways. For now, we'll make just one block.

You will need two templates—triangle C and square E. Use four different fabrics—three solids and one print. On the *wrong* side of the fabric, trace:

C — 4 of solid color No. 1
C — 4 of solid color No. 2
E — 10 of solid color No. 3
E — 10 of print

In the design (Fig. 23), note that five of the nine squares are subdivided into checkerboard squares. The remaining squares are divided into triangles. When you trace the triangles, be sure to place the longest side on the straight of the fabric, as shown in Fig. 12, page 20.

Cut the pieces, adding ½" seam allowances, and follow the same general pin-basting and sewing instructions given for Shoofly, on page 20.

Arrange the pieces in front of you to follow the design in Fig. 23. As you finish a seam or section, return it to its position. You would be amazed at how the pieces can get mixed up.

First join pieces to form the nine basic squares, then make the three rows. Finally, join the rows to form the block. Be particularly careful when you pin rows at seam lines. Try to match all corner points.

OHIO STAR

This design, often called Variable Star, is the last nine-patch block. We think of it as the queen of nine-patch designs because it's beautiful and also one of the most challenging to make. You will be working with small triangles, and it's easy to get them turned in the wrong direction. So, keep an eye on Fig. 24 as you work.

The Ohio Star uses two templates, square A and triangle D, and three fabrics. Choose two solid colors and one print. On the *wrong* side of the fabric, trace and cut (adding ½" seam allowances):

A — 4 of solid color No. 1
A — 1 of print
D — 4 of solid color No. 1
D — 4 of solid color No. 2
D — 8 of print

Arrange all pieces for the block, right side up, according to Fig. 24.

Keep the pieces in front of you as you work, and pick them up one at a time. The successful piecing of this pattern depends upon careful pinning, particularly at the intersections.

Start with the top row. To complete the center square (top row), you must join four triangles. First sew one print triangle to a solid color triangle. Open this, and you have one large triangle as in Fig. 25. Next, join the two remaining triangles (a print and a solid) to make a second large triangle. Now join the two large triangles to make the square (Fig. 26). Repeat these steps to complete three more squares.

Make the rows, and finally, the block. Keep your eye on Fig. 24 and be careful. This one is tricky.

ONE-OF-A-KIND BLOCK

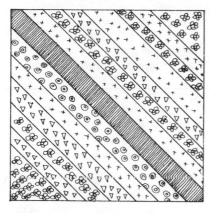

Fig. 27   String

(See also plate 3)

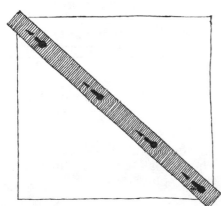

Fig. 28   Placing first strip

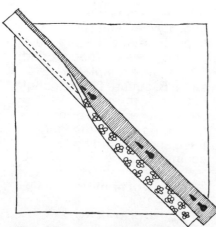

Fig. 29   Stitching second strip

Here's a pieced-work design that doesn't fit neatly into a category like the nine-patch blocks you've made. In fact, it doesn't fit into any grouping. We think you'll enjoy doing this for a change of pace.

STRING

Look at the design in Fig. 27, and you can understand the name. This patchwork block is made of strips (wide strings) of fabric stitched to a square of foundation fabric. There's no rule about the width of strips, so you can mix wide and narrow ones. Just try to place contrasting fabrics next to each other. Note that the strips decrease in length as they move away from the center. It's a good design for using odds and ends.

For the foundation square, inexpensive muslin works well. What's more, the fabric is in keeping with the scrap-bag beginnings of this design.

To mark the foundation fabric, you could simply measure off a 15″ square on muslin. However, we suggest you first make a template of cardboard or posterboard that is exactly 15″ square. Then you will have a handy template you can use again when you come to the appliqué designs later in the book. Use your T-square ruler or triangle to make the corners perfectly square.

Place the 15″-square template on the *wrong* side of the foundation fabric and trace around it. Cut out the block, adding ½″ seam allowances.

For the design, cut one strip of fabric (on the straight grain), about 23″ long and 2″ wide. Place this strip, *right side up*, diagonally across the right side of the foundation square, running from the top left corner to the bottom right corner, as in Fig. 28. Anchor the strip in place with a row of pins down the center. Don't sew anything yet.

Cut a second strip. Place it on top of the first strip, *right side down*. Keep the strips even at the lower edge. Pin in place, then stitch the two strips together along the lower edge, catching them to the foundation square. Turn the top strip to the right side, covering the raw seam as you do, as in Fig. 29. Finger-press along the seam line.

Cut a third strip. Place this on top of the first (center) strip, *right side down*. Keep strips even along the upper edge. Pin and stitch as you did the first seam.

Continue to add strips, working away from the center, until the foundation piece is completely covered. Use shorter lengths as you work toward the corners. When the block is completed, trim away excess fabric at the edges.

FOUR-PATCH BLOCKS

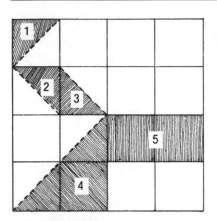

Fig. 30 Basic four-patch block

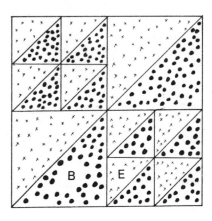

Fig. 31 Flock of Geese
(See also plate 3)

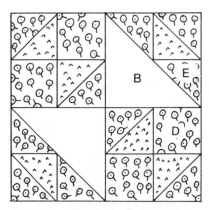

Fig. 32 Old Maid's Puzzle
(See also plate 3)

The name of this group may lead you to believe that these designs are easier than nine-patches. However, you will find that many four-patch designs have more pieces to be stitched together.

The four-patch is often based on a block divided into 16 small squares, not just four (see Fig. 30).

You can produce hundreds of patterns from this basic block, and the broken lines show you some of the possibilities. The broken lines also illustrate how you can cut a large section as one unit, rather than piecing all the small sections together.

Look at the shaded areas. Triangles 1, 2 and 3 would all be cut as individual shapes, then pieced together. Triangle 4, however, can be cut as one large triangle—and generally is. Also, rectangle 5 can be cut as one long piece, rather than in two sections. You will find this happening as you make the four-patch blocks. Of course, you don't have to make decisions about what to cut large or small. The patterns are the correct size.

First, make templates for all the four-patch pattern pieces on page 31. (Directions for making templates are on page 19 if you want to review them.)

You should have five four-patch templates. Label each one. *Note:* Some of the triangles will be used later for another design called Twenty Triangles.

FLOCK OF GEESE

This four-patch block (Fig. 31) reflects an unknown co-lonial woman's awareness of nature. She watched migrating birds and translated their wedge-shaped flying formations into this intriguing patchwork design.

Use two templates—triangle B and triangle E. Select two print fabrics—one light and one dark. On the *wrong* side of the fabric, trace and cut (adding ½" seam allowances):

B — 2 of light print
B — 2 of dark print
E — 8 of light print
E — 8 of dark print

Arrange the pieces in front of you, right side up. Begin by joining the two large triangles at the upper right to make one large square. Repeat with the two large triangles at lower left.

Join the small triangles to form small squares, then join the four squares at upper left to form one large square. Repeat to make a large square at lower right.

Join the two top large squares and the two bottom large squares. Finally, stitch the top half to the bottom half to complete the block.

OLD MAID'S PUZZLE

Here's a very old pattern (Fig. 32) that really is a puzzle to put together. It's easy to get the pieces turned around.

Use three templates—triangle B, square D and triangle E. Choose three fabrics—one solid color and two prints. On the *wrong* side of the fabric, trace and cut (adding ½" seam allowances):

B — 2 of solid color
D — 4 of print No. 1
E — 10 of print No. 1
E — 6 of print No. 2

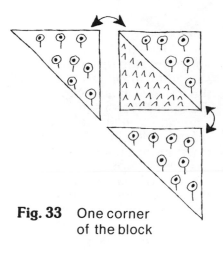

Fig. 33 One corner of the block

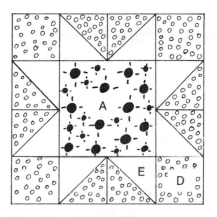

Fig. 34 Sawtooth
(See also plate 3)

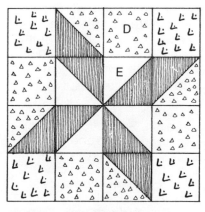

Fig. 35 Clay's Choice
(See also plate 6)

Place the pieces in front of you, right side up, following Fig. 32. First, join the small print triangles to form six small squares. (You will have some triangles left over.)

Next, work with the pieces in the upper right corner—a small square and two small triangles (Fig. 33). Join these pieces to make one large triangle. Then stitch this triangle to the solid color triangle B to form a large square. Repeat to complete a large square at lower left.

Work with the four small squares at upper left. Join these squares to make one large square. Repeat to complete a large square at lower right.

Join the two large squares at the top, and the two large squares at the bottom. Finally, stitch the top half to the bottom half to complete the block.

SAWTOOTH

This pattern (Fig. 34) was used by Native Americans in many of their rug designs. The colonists gave it this name because it resembled a saw, a necessary piece of equipment in their households. The star design is the basis of more complicated patchwork patterns.

Use three templates—large square A, small square D and small triangle E. Choose three fabrics—one solid color and two prints. On the *wrong* side of the fabric, trace and cut (adding ½″ seam allowances):

    A — 1 of print No. 1
    D — 4 of print No. 2
    E — 8 of solid color
    E — 8 of print No. 2

Arrange all the pieces of the pattern in front of you, right side up. Watch the placement of each triangle and refer to Fig. 34.

First join the triangles to form small squares. Then join all the squares in the top row, and the squares in the bottom row.

Join the two remaining small squares (placed vertically) on the right, and the two remaining small squares (placed vertically) on the left. Next, add these side pieces to the large center square to form a center section. Finally, stitch the top and bottom rows to the center section.

CLAY'S CHOICE

Henry Clay was once asked to judge a quilt contest. He chose a quilt made with this unnamed design (Fig. 35) as the winner. From that time on, it was known as Clay's Choice. The pattern probably reminds you of a pinwheel.

Use two templates—square D and triangle E. Choose four fabrics—two solid colors and two prints. On the *wrong* side of the fabric, trace and cut (adding ½″ seam allowances):

    D — 4 of print No. 1
    D — 4 of print No. 2
    E — 4 of solid color No. 1
    E — 8 of solid color No. 2
    E — 4 of print No. 1

Place the pieces in front of you. Join the triangles to make squares, then join the squares to form rows. Finally, stitch the rows together to complete the block.

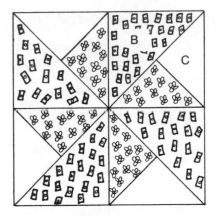

Fig. 36 Windmill
(See also plate 6)

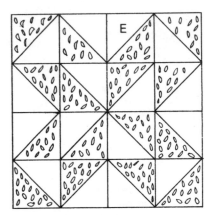

Fig. 37 Pieced Star
(See also plate 6)

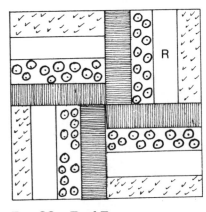

Fig. 38 Rail Fence
(See also plate 6)

WINDMILL

Windmills were (and still are) used as an energy source on some farms, and they provided the inspiration for this particular design (Fig. 36).

The block uses only triangles, and you'll have to watch the design as you work. It's easy to mix up the triangles as you sew them together.

Use two templates, triangle B and triangle C, and three fabrics. Choose a solid color and two prints. On the *wrong* side of the fabric, trace and cut (adding ½" seam allowances):

B — 4 of print No. 1
C — 4 of solid color
C — 4 of print No. 2

Arrange all the pieces in front of you, right side up. First, join the C triangles to make larger triangles. Then join the large triangles to form four squares.

Join the two top squares and the two bottom squares. Finally, sew the top section to the bottom section to complete the block.

PIECED STAR

This is one of the outstanding star patterns (Fig. 37). It was devised to make use of small pieces of fabric and is very effective when made in fabrics with a strong contrast. This is another block made entirely of triangles. Watch the placement carefully.

To make this design, use only one template—triangle E. Select two fabrics—one solid color and one print. On the *wrong* side of the fabric, trace and cut (adding ½" seam allowances):

E — 16 of solid color

E — 16 of print

Keep the pieces in front of you, right side up, arranged according to Fig. 37. Begin at the top row, and piece triangles to form squares. Continue with the second row, then the third and fourth rows, always joining triangles to form squares.

Next, join all the squares in the top row. Repeat to complete the remaining rows.

Join the top row to the second row. Finally, add the remaining rows to complete the block.

RAIL FENCE

The design in Fig. 38 is often set as a continuous pattern (without sashing), and it is not a typical four-patch design. We've simply taken four basic units and put them together to create a four-patch block. That's why we put it at the end of this section, even though it is easier to make than most of the four-patch designs you have already completed.

Rail Fence is a very old pattern, reminiscent of fences used in New England to form precise outlines of adjoining farms. Like the String block, this design needs only narrow strips of fabric.

Use only one template—rectangle R (pattern is on page 32). Select four fabrics—two solid colors and two prints. On the *wrong* side of the fabric, trace and cut (adding ½" seam allowances):

R — 4 of solid color No. 1
R — 4 of solid color No. 2
R — 4 of print No. 1
R — 4 of print No. 2

Line up four rectangles—one of each fabric—in an order that pleases you. Stitch them together to form a square. Arrange the remaining fabric pieces in the same order and complete three more squares.

Position the squares according to Fig. 38. Join the two top squares, then the two bottom squares. Finally, stitch the top section to the bottom section to complete the block.

ONE FINAL PIECED BLOCK

So far we've divided our 15″ squares into nine-patches and four-patches, and made a String block. Here's another design that shows the endless possibilities of patchwork. It's a block carved up to form a series of diminishing squares.

TWENTY TRIANGLES

There's a special reason for making the block shown in Fig. 39. Each quilt deserves to be dated and signed by its maker. You'll put a lot of time and effort into planning and making your quilt, and it may well become an heirloom. It is conceivable that your quilt will have a life span of 200 or more years. Imagine the joy of the quilt enthusiast eight generations down the line who discovers your quilt in a trunk or on a bed and is spared the difficulty of identifying its age and maker.

The smallest middle square in this block is the signature space. You may embroider your name and date there when you make the block, or you can quilt them in later.

You need six templates, but you only have to make three new ones. Use three triangles, B, C and E that you made for the four-patch

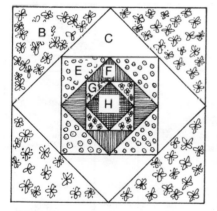

Fig. 39   Twenty Triangles

(See also plate 6)

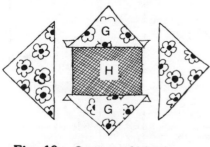

Fig. 40   Center of block

designs. Then add triangles F and G, and square H from patterns on page 32.

Choose six coordinated fabrics, three solid colors and three prints. Decide how you will arrange them by studying Fig. 39.

On the *wrong* side of the fabric, trace and cut (adding ½″ seam allowances):

B — 4 of print No. 1
C — 4 of solid color No. 1
E — 4 of print No. 2
F — 4 of solid color No. 2
G — 4 of print No. 3
H — 1 of solid color No. 3

Assemble the pieces in front of you, looking at Fig. 39. Take square H, and add one triangle G to the top, and one triangle G to the bottom (Fig. 40). Then add a triangle G to the right side and another to the left side. Continue to build the block by adding triangles in the same manner, working away from the center until the block is completed.

If you want to embroider your name and the date, do it now. You can use the chain stitch described on page 48. If you would rather quilt your name and date, pencil them on the block with a No. 5H or No. 6H (hard) pencil. This will guide your tiny quilting stitches when you put the quilt together later on.

Would you believe it? You have completed 12 sampler blocks. We've found that this is a good place to break in and do a little quilting. You don't have enough blocks for a big quilt yet, but you can make a miniature quilt. We'll tell you how in the next chapter.

Some reminders

1. Be as accurate as possible when you draft templates.

2. Trace pattern templates for pieced work on the wrong side of the fabric.

3. Place edges of squares and rectangles on the straight grain. Place the longest side of a triangle on the straight grain.

4. Sharpen your pencil frequently when you are tracing templates on fabric.

5. Add ½" seam allowances when you cut out fabric pieces and blocks. Trim them to just under ¼" after each seam is stitched.

6. Arrange all pieces of a quilt block, right side up, to form the design, then begin to sew them together.

7. Follow these basic steps: trace, cut, pin-baste, stitch, trim, finger-press.

Patterns

NINE-PATCH

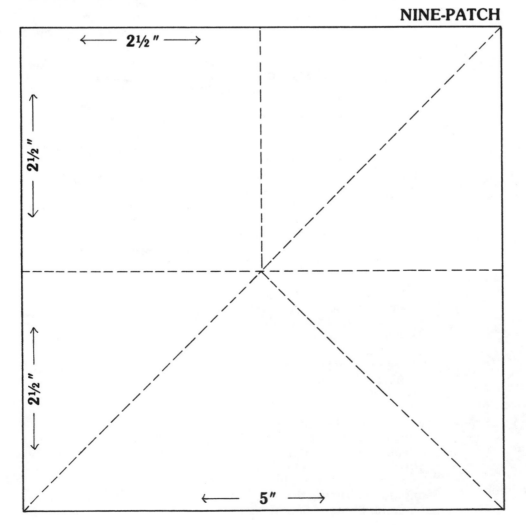

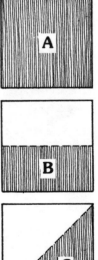

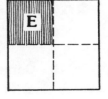

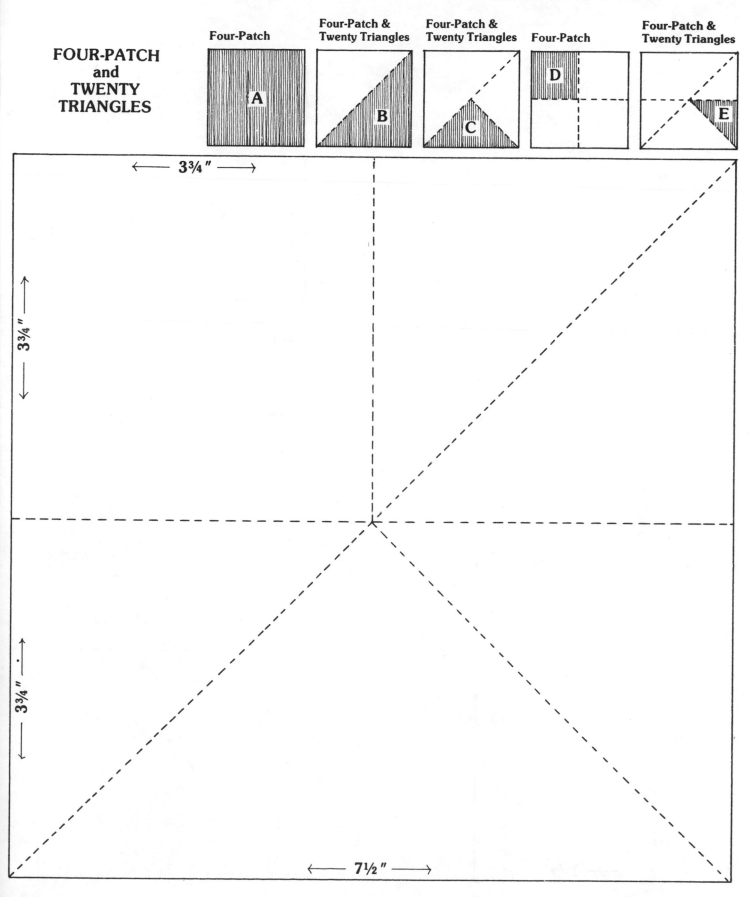

FOUR-PATCH and TWENTY TRIANGLES

Four-Patch
A

Four-Patch & Twenty Triangles
B

Four-Patch & Twenty Triangles
C

Four-Patch
D

Four-Patch & Twenty Triangles
E

← 3¾ " →

3¾ "

3¾ "

← 7½ " →

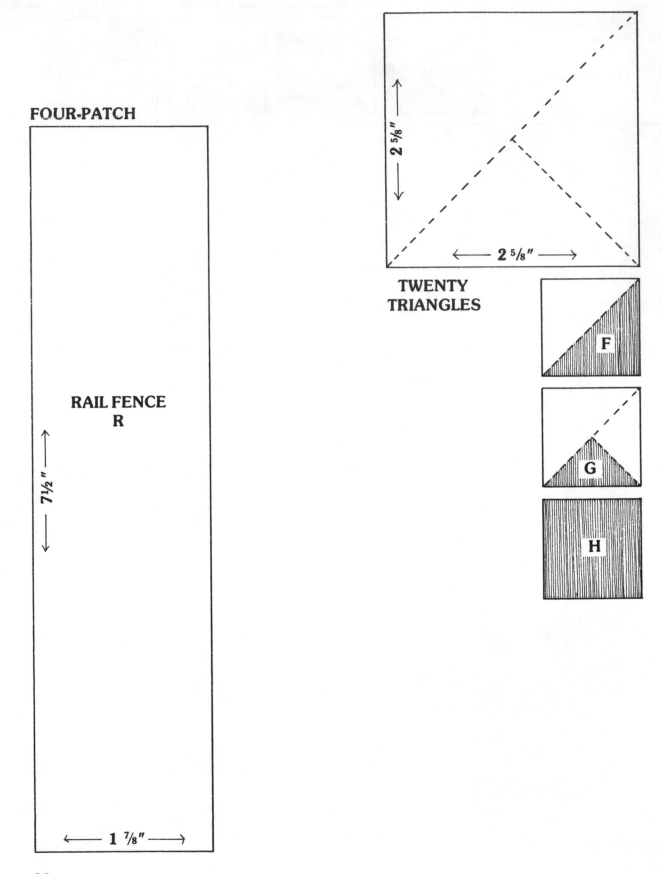

FOUR-PATCH

**RAIL FENCE
R**

7½"

1 ⅞"

2 ⅝"

2 ⅝"

**TWENTY
TRIANGLES**

F

G

H

Plate 1

Beginner's Sampler Quilt with
20 patchwork blocks.
By Jessie MacDonald.

Beginner's blocks

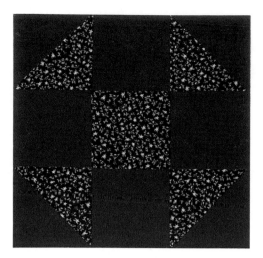

Shoofly

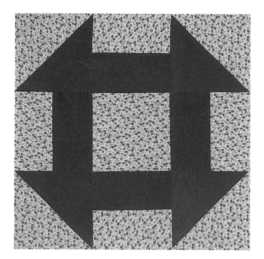

Churn Dash

Greek Cross

Arrange fabrics so that patchwork design separates from the sashing, as at left.

Plate 2

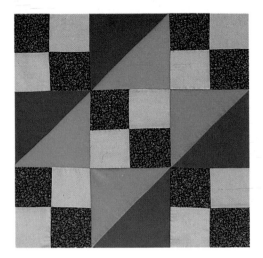

Jacob's Ladder

Ohio Star

String

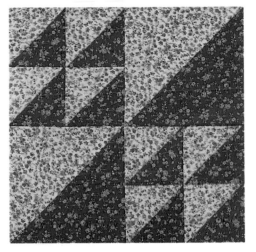

Flock of Geese

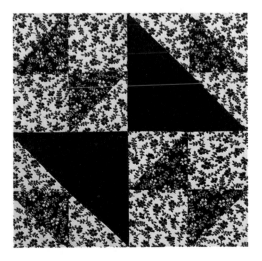

Old Maid's Puzzle

Sawtooth

Plate 3

Pillows make decorative use of your favorite patchwork blocks.
Chapter 4 tells you how to complete the quilted pillow shown in the foreground.

Plate 5

Quilt using a single design
(Grandmother's Flower Garden),
set with sashing.
By Pauline Killen.

Beginner's blocks

Clay's Choice

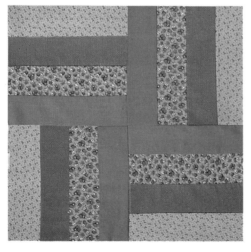

Windmill

Pieced Star

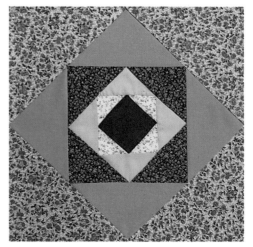

Rail Fence

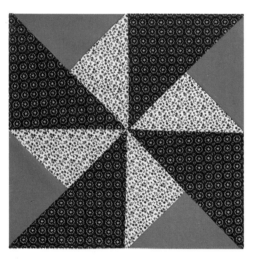

Twenty Triangles

Plate 6

Pieced block for pillow

Heart

Lancaster Rose

Tulip

Jean's Rose

Honey Bee

Plate 7

Crib quilts using single designs (Heart, below, and Ohio Star, right), set with sashing. By Karen Mikle.

Plate 8

4 Complete a miniature quilt –a pillow

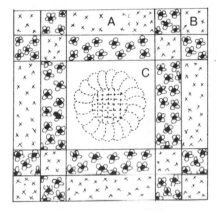

Fig. 41   Block for pillow
with quilted center
(See also plate 7)

When we suggest that students stop working on sample patches and take time out to make a pillow, we hear loud groans. No one wants to make a *pillow* when everyone is anxious to make a *quilt*.

However, the pillow we propose in Fig. 41 is not an ordinary one. It gives you actual quilting experience on a small scale. Those broken lines in the center square indicate quilting stitches that form a design called Single Feathered Plate—a design used by the Chinese and Persians before 1 B.C.

You also learn how to transfer a quilting design to fabric and how to set the center square in sashing (double sashing, in this case).

The finished pillow top is stitched to a two-piece back section to make a pillow cover. An inner pillow can be slipped inside—and we tell you how to make the inner pillow, too.

Students who complain about this little detour often confess later that the lesson comes in handy when they assemble their quilts. Some women like the design so much that they make another Single Feathered Plate block for their Beginner's Sampler Quilt. You may want to do the

same for your quilt.

We strongly recommend that you read this entire chapter before you cut any fabric. There are detailed directions for certain techniques, along with the reasons you should use them. You will find it easier to handle the work if you've read the whole sequence ahead of time.

Supplies

For this design block, you should make three templates—two squares and a rectangle. Copy the pattern pieces beginning on page 38.

When you make the large square C template, you must also copy the quilting design exactly in the center. To do this, first use dressmaker's carbon paper to trace the design onto your posterboard or cardboard. Then take a felt-tip pen (with a fine line), and carefully go over the design to make darker lines.

Select three fabrics for the block—two prints of contrasting values and a light solid color. You should have enough fabric to make the block and the two-piece backing. It's nice if the solid color is a cotton-polyester blend because the fabric's slight sheen will help show off your

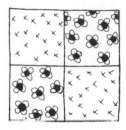

Fig. 42 Forming a corner

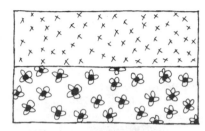

Fig. 43 Forming the sides

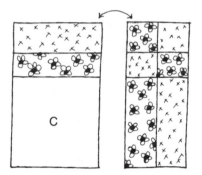

Fig. 44 Begin piecing the block

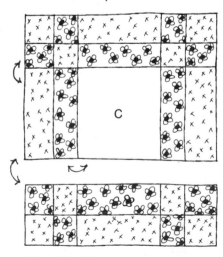

Fig. 45 Finish piecing the block

quilting stitches. However, all-cotton fabric is fine.

You will need to assemble these additional supplies:

• *Batting,* 16" square. Use polyester bonded batting. You can buy a small package (45x60") which is used for a crib quilt. This gives you enough batting to quilt six pillow tops.

• *Muslin* or any other soft cotton fabric for the insides of the pillow (it won't show). Cut three 16" squares. One is for backing the pillow top when you quilt it; two additional squares are used to make the inner pillow.

• *Quilting needles* (Betweens size 7 or 8).

• *Quilting thread* to match the light-colored center block C. The Feathered Plate design is particularly beautiful done in matching thread. What's more, using the same color thread helps minimize any unevenness in your quilting stitches.

• *Polyester fiberfill* for stuffing the inner pillow (a 1-lb. package is enough for two pillows).

• *Corded piping,* 2 yd., for the edge of the pillow cover (optional).

Piecing the block

Use your templates to trace:

    A— 4 of light print
    A— 4 of darker print
    B— 8 of light print
    B— 8 of darker print
    C— 1 of light solid color

Place each template on the *wrong* side of the fabric and trace around it. Cut out the pieces, adding ½" seam allowances on all sides. Arrange the pieces in front of you, right side up (see Fig. 41). Use our trusty pin-baste, stitch, trim and finger-press method. (Turn back to page 20 if you need to review this.) Assemble the block in this order:

1. Join four B pieces to complete a corner square (Fig. 42). Complete the other three corner squares.

2. Join a dark print A to a light print A to form a larger rectangle (Fig. 43). Complete three more of these rectangles.

3. Sew one rectangle to the top of center square C, with the darker print next to C, as in Fig. 44.

4. Sew one corner square to a second rectangle (Fig. 44), being sure that dark edges meet light edges as shown. Then sew this unit to the center section.

5. Sew another corner square to a third rectangle, and add this unit to the center section (Fig. 45).

6. Sew the two remaining corner squares to the remaining rectangle to form the bottom unit. Then add this to the center section.

Have it all together? Good!

Transferring the design

Now, take the C template and place it under the center square of your block. What do you see? The Feathered Plate design! This is your reward for carefully copying the quilting pattern onto your template.

Center the template exactly. Turn the pillow top over and anchor the template to the fabric with strips of masking tape. This will prevent the template from slipping as you trace the design.

Work on the right side of the fabric with a sharp No. 5H or No. 6H pencil. (Be sure you use a hard pencil that won't smear.) Trace the lines lightly, but make them clear enough so you will be able to follow them as you quilt. Turn the block over again and remove the template and masking tape.

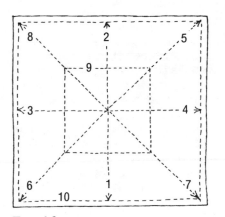

Fig. 46 Basting lines

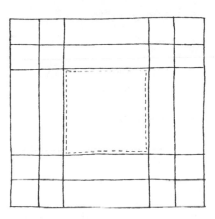

Fig. 47 First line of quilting

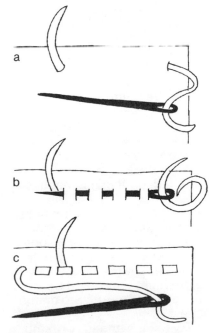

Fig. 48 Anchoring thread
without knot

Machine-stitch all around the edge of the block, working on the wrong side and stitching on top of the pencil lines. This stitching will show on both sides of the fabric and will be your guide when you quilt the outside edge of the pillow top.

Stacking and basting

Pin the pillow top sandwich together, with the design block on top (right side up), a 16" square of batting in the middle and a 16" square of muslin (or other cotton fabric) on the bottom. Now you are ready to baste.

"Baste?" you say. "I hate to baste!" The only consolation we can offer is to guarantee that when you eventually remove all the basting threads, your pillow top will be evenly quilted. This more than compensates for the effort you expend in doing a boring—but necessary—chore. The alternative is to settle for an off-center design, uneven quilting stitches and batting that has bunched in spots.

For basting, use a single strand of white mercerized cotton with a knot at one end. (Dark thread tends to leave colored marks on the fabric underneath the knots. When you remove the basting threads, dark dots may remain.)

Begin basting at the center of the pillow top, and refer to Fig. 46. The basting lines are numbered to show the order that you should follow. Always work from the center to the outside, and make your basting stitches about 1" long.

First baste from the center to the outside edges along the straight grain (Lines 1-2-3-4). Then baste from the center to the outside corners (Lines 5-6-7-8).

Next, baste around the center square on the seam line (Line 9). Finally, baste all around the outside edge directly over the line you stitched earlier (Line 10).

When you finish, the three layers are enclosed. You have a neat little package, and the layers will not shift as you work.

Now you are ready to begin the quilting stitch described below. Your first line of quilting will outline the center square, about ¼" inside the seam lines (Fig. 47).

Quilting stitches, no knots

The quilting stitch is the running stitch (Fig. 14), and the uniformity of your stitches is more important than the length. With practice, you should be able to produce six to eight stitches to the inch. As you learn to work faster, you'll find it becomes easier to make the stitches both smaller and more uniform. Eventually you will develop your own style of quilting. It is almost like your signature.

Since the back of your work should be as beautiful as the front, no knots must show. We always work with unknotted thread for quilting. Some quilters hide their knots in the batting, but we find that this tends to create tiny lumps. So try our method of beginning a new length of thread—without a knot— following Fig. 48. (We realize the back of the pillow top won't show, but this is practice for your quilt, so let's do it the right way.)

After you thread the needle, moisten about 2" of the long end of your thread. (This makes the thread swell so that it will be easier to anchor.) Take one long stitch with the needle piercing the top fabric, then running through the batting the length of the needle before you bring

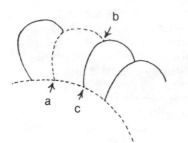

Fig. 49   Quilting the swirls

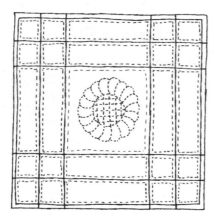

Fig. 50   Quilting inside all seam lines

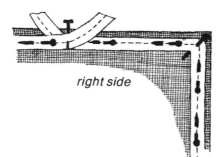

right side

Fig. 51   Adding the piping

it back up (a). Pull the thread through the fabric, leaving a tail about 1" long.

Turn the needle around and begin a running stitch back to the point of entry (b), going through all three layers with each stitch. Try to gather two or more stitches on your needle at one time.

These stitches should catch the buried thread. After you make a few more stitches (c), pull the thread gently to make sure that it has been anchored and won't pull out. Then snip off the tail.

Continue quilting until the thread needs replacing. Finish a length of thread the same way you started it—by burying it in the batting. Insert your needle into the top fabric, run it through the batting under the quilting line, and come up a needle's length *ahead.* Leave a short tail.

Start the next thread at this tail, going back through the batting to the last quilting stitch. Then turn the needle around and quilt over the two buried threads. Cut off the tails after you have stitched over them and are sure the new thread is secure.

Using your fingers

As you quilt, grasp the fabric with your left hand. (If you are left-handed, use your right hand to hold the fabric.) Keep your thumb on top of the block and your fingers underneath. Hold the bulk of the fabric in the palm of your hand.

Each time you insert the needle to make a new stitch, graze the top of the index or middle finger on your left hand to make sure that your needle has penetrated all thicknesses of the quilt. (It isn't easy to quilt a sandwich.)

We may as well tell you that your fingers will become

tender. As you continue to quilt, they will develop callouses. You can remedy this somewhat by putting strips of transparent tape over the fingertips of your left hand (trim off the excess tape).

Wear a thimble on the middle finger of your right hand. If you are unaccustomed to using a thimble, put it on anyway. After a short time, you will find you can adjust to its presence. There will be great consolation for all this "pain and suffering" when you show the finished work to your family and friends.

Quilting the design

After you complete a single row of stitches around the inside of the center square (Fig. 47), you are ready to do the Feathered Plate. Don't cut the thread. Take a tiny backstitch (Fig. 15). Dip your needle into the batting and bring it up on the circle of the Feathered Plate.

Quilt around the circle. Then begin the outside swirls (Fig. 49) by bringing your needle up at the base of one swirl (a). Quilt to where this swirl meets the next swirl (b). Slip the needle into the batting at this point and bring it out at the base of the next swirl (c). Continue quilting all the swirls.

Next, quilt all the horizontal and vertical lines in the center of the Plate.

After the Feathered Plate is finished, quilt inside each piece of sashing (Fig. 50), about ¼" from the seam lines. Do not catch seam allowances in your stitches. (You'll soon discover why we urge you to trim your seams as you sew. Otherwise, you would be trying to quilt through too many layers.)

Try to plan ahead, working from one area to another close by, so that you don't waste thread moving from one section to another. Every time you end a thread and start a new one, you weaken the construction of the quilt. The fewer starts and stops you make, the better.

Another rule to remember is: Work from the center to the outside in gradually enlarging areas. For example, do the center of the pillow, then quilt the area surrounding it (the inside rows of sashing). Then work on the next surrounding area (the outside rows of sashing). In this way, you quilt evenly from the center toward all the outside edges.

When you get to the last row of quilting—around the outside edge—you will see why we suggested you put a row of machine stitching there. Without it, you would have no guide to show you where to quilt.

...Finished quilting? It's time to snip the basting threads and pull them out. You have completed a miniature quilt! Isn't it beautiful? And wasn't it worth taking the time to put in the basting threads?

Optional edging

If you wish to use a corded piping on the edge of the pillow cover, add it now. This step is optional, and you may want to skip it.

To add corded piping, place the corded edge toward the center of the block, and the seam allowance of the piping along the outside edge of the block.

Pin the piping around the outside edge, beginning at the center of one side. Place pins on the seamline, going through the stitching on the piping and through the stitching around the outside edge of the pillow top (Fig. 51). Insert pins from right to left as illustrated so the pins can be

removed easily as you stitch. Ease the piping around the corners, placing one pin perpendicular at each corner. Finish by overlapping the piping; let both ends run off the edge of the block. Stitch the piping in place, using a zipper foot (or cording foot), and removing the pins as you go.

Note: A ruffle may be added in the same manner.

Making the pillow cover

Your miniature quilt is ready to be turned into a quilted pillow cover. For this, you make a two-piece back section. This overlaps so that an inner pillow can be slipped inside without the bother of a zipper.

Cut two pieces of fabric 11x16". (You have enough extra of your border print for this.) On each piece, along a 16" length, make a ¼" turn to the wrong side. Make a second turn, also ¼", to form a hem, and stitch (Fig. 52).

To assemble the pillow covering, place the quilted pillow top on a table, right side up. On top of this, place the back sections, right sides down, and with the two hems running horizontally across the center (Fig. 53). Keep raw edges of the layers even (the hems across the back sections will overlap).

Insert a few pins along the edges to anchor the layers, then turn the fabric over so the quilted section is on top (wrong side out). Pin the layers together, inserting pins perpendicular to the fabric edges. Machine-stitch around the block, directly on top of the previous stitching. Turn the pillow cover right side out.

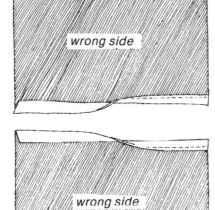

wrong side

wrong side

Fig. 52   Hemming the back sections

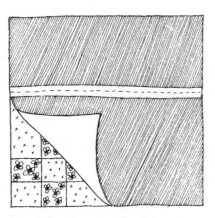

Fig. 53   Sewing back sections to front

Making the inner pillow

The inner pillow holds the stuffing and never shows—it's inside your fancy pillow cover.

Sew two 16" squares of muslin (or other cotton fabric) with right sides together. Use ½" seam allowances and leave a 5" opening on one side for turning. Turn the fabric right side out and stuff with polyester fiberfill until the pillow is firm. Close the opening with small hand stitches.

Insert this inner pillow into the pillow covering. There! You have a quilted pillow—and a lot of information you can use later.

Patterns

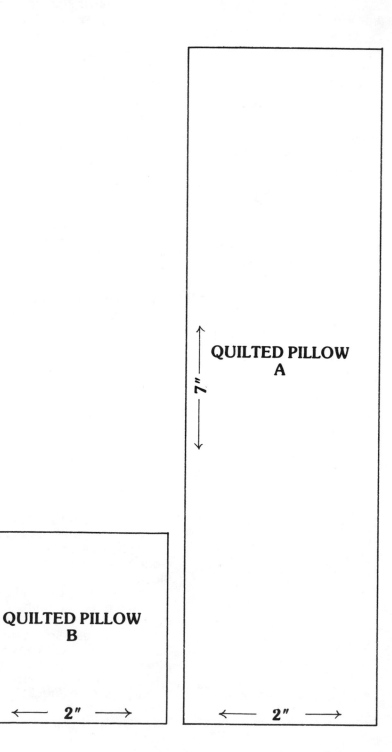

QUILTED PILLOW
A

7"

2"

QUILTED PILLOW
B

2"

2"

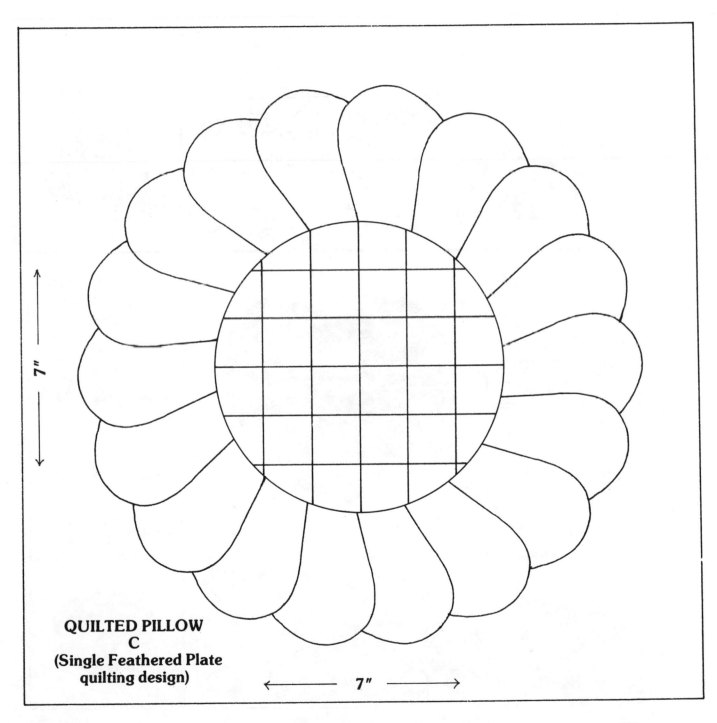

**QUILTED PILLOW
C
(Single Feathered Plate
quilting design)**

7"

7"

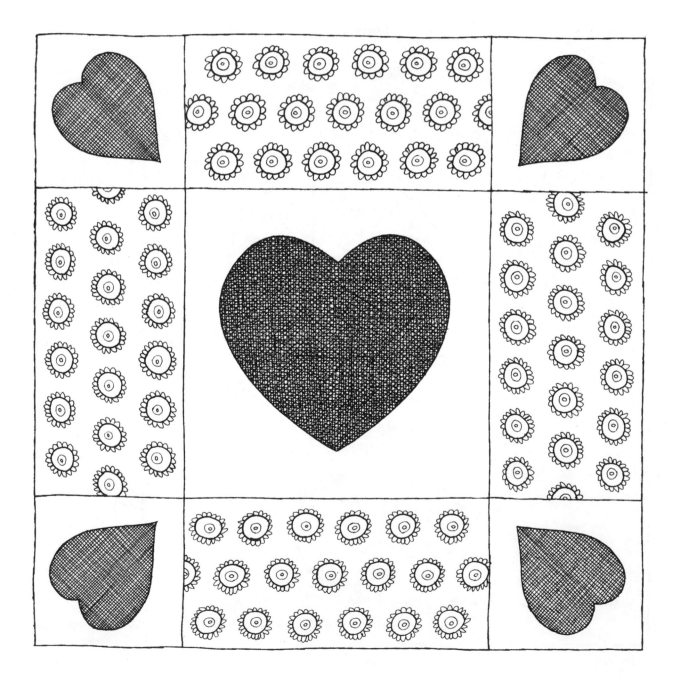

5 Now try appliqué

Appliqué is an ornamental effect produced by cutting pieces of one fabric and sewing them to the surface of another fabric. Happy was the pioneer woman who finally gathered enough yard goods and time to indulge herself in the art of appliqué. This form of quilt-making gives you the opportunity to draw pictures, using fabric as a medium.

PLAIN APPLIQUÉ

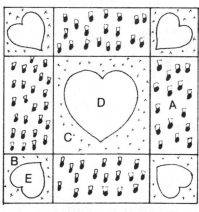

Fig. 54 Heart
(See also plate 7)

We'll start with a simple design that has only a single layer of appliqué, the Heart. Next is the Lancaster Rose, which uses two layers of appliqué, with some overlapping pieces. These blocks introduce a new stitch—the appliqué stitch. They also introduce a new rule: For most appliqué, trace the template on the *right* side of the fabric, so you can see the lines when you turn the seam allowance under. Also, have center of design run along straight grain.

HEART

For this block (Fig. 54), a large heart is sewed to the center square, then framed with sashing. The four small hearts in the corner squares can be appliquéd, as in our sample (see plate 7). Or the designs can be quilted later.

Make the five templates from the patterns beginning on page 51, and label them. (How-to directions for making templates are on page 19.) Select three fabrics—one solid color and two prints.

On the *wrong* side of the fabric, trace and cut (adding ½" seam allowances):

    A—4 of print No. 1
    B—4 of print No. 2
    C—1 of print No. 2

On the *right* side of the fabric, trace and cut (adding ½" seam allowances):

    D—1 of solid color
    E—4 of solid color (if you wish to appliqué the corner hearts)

Preparing the appliqué

First put a line of stay-stitching around the large heart D, just outside the pencil lines (Fig. 55). This will hold the shape as you work and help you turn the edges evenly. Use machine stitching or tiny hand stitches.

Then slash the fabric to, but not through, the stitching line along the curves. Slashes are necessary at the top inside curve so the fabric can spread open as it folds to the wrong

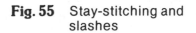
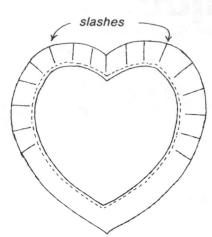

Fig. 55 Stay-stitching and slashes

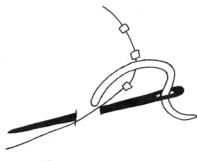

Fig. 56 Appliqué stitch

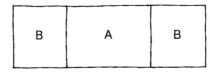

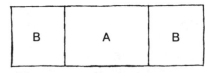

Fig. 57 Piecing the block

side. The slashes around the outside curves let excess fabric overlap for a neat finish as it turns to the wrong side.

Turn the raw edge under along the pencil line so that the stitching is hidden, and baste along the turned edge. Press with an iron.

(An alternative method is to skip the stitching and slash the fabric almost to the pencil line. Center the template on the wrong side of the fabric and iron the seam allowance over it. Remove the template and baste along the turned edge. This method does save stitching, but you must be careful not to burn your fingers since you have to work close to the edge of the iron.)

Trim the seam allowance to 1/8" to remove excess fabric. If your fabric is heavy or if this is your first appliqué, trim to just under ¼". Beginners find it easier to have that extra bit of fabric to work with.

Positioning the appliqué

Now you are ready to appliqué. Center heart D in the middle of foundation square C. Find the centers by folding the square in half vertically, and then folding the heart down the center vertically. Position the heart on the square, lining up the center folds; keep the heart evenly spaced between the top and bottom of the square. Pin and baste in place.

Use a needle with a single strand of thread in a color to match the heart. Knot one end of the thread, and begin the appliqué stitch described below to attach the heart.

The appliqué stitch

Bring the needle and thread through from the wrong side of the block, letting the needle pierce the appliqué design at the folded edge.

Begin the next stitch on the foundation fabric (Fig. 56). Insert the needle diagonally into the foundation fabric (close to where the thread emerged), and bring it out 1/8" ahead to pierce the fold of the appliqué. Continue in this manner, trying to keep your stitches even and as invisible as possible. A slanting stitch will appear on the back of the foundation fabric.

Finishing the block

When the heart is attached, remove the basting threads. Add the sashing, according to Fig. 57. Follow the construction method you used for pieced work—pin-baste, stitch, trim and finger-press.

Make the top row by joining a corner square B to each side of a rectangle A. Repeat to make the bottom row. Add a rectangle A to each side of the center square. Finally, stitch the top and bottom rows to the center section to complete the block.

If you choose to appliqué heart patterns E to the corner squares B, do it now. Follow the directions you used for appliquéing the large heart. If you prefer to quilt the small heart designs, position the template E on each corner square (on top of the fabric) and trace around it with a No. 5H or No. 6H pencil. (Use a yellow pencil on dark fabric.) These lines will be quilted later.

LANCASTER ROSE

Now that you have learned the basic appliqué technique, let's try a slightly more complicated pattern called Lancaster Rose. Look at Fig. 58, and select a color combination that appeals to you. Choose four fabrics—two

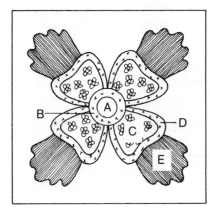

Fig. 58 Lancaster Rose
(See also plate 7)

solid colors and two prints.

Make five templates from the patterns on page 53, and label them. You also will need the 15"-square template that you made in Chapter 1 for the String block.

On the *right* side of the fabric, trace and cut (adding ½" seam allowances):

    A— 1 of print No. 1
    B— 1 of print No. 2
    C— 4 of print No. 1
    D— 4 of print No. 2
    E— 4 of solid color No. 1

On the *wrong* side of the fabric, trace and cut (adding ½" seam allowances):

    15" square — 1 of solid color No. 2

To work with the curved shapes, follow the same directions given for the Heart appliqué. Outline the shapes with stay stitching (machine stitching or small hand stitches) just outside the pencil lines. Slash to the stitching line around the curved areas and into the dips of curves. Turn the raw edges to the wrong side so the stitching is hidden. Baste along the edges, press with an iron, and trim the excess seam allowances.

Centering this design is more complicated. To find the exact center of the foundation block, fold the block in half, first along the grain lines vertically, then horizontally. Then fold the block diagonally both ways. Finger-press all the folds as you work.

Arrange the appliqué pieces in front of you. First center the large heart-shaped pieces D along the diagonal folds of the foundation block, with their small ends touching at the center of the block, and pin in place.

Center the smaller heart-shaped C pieces on top of the D pieces, and pin. Tuck the leaves E under the hearts, centering them on the diagonal folds.

Cover the center of the block with large circle B, then position the small circle A on top. Pin and baste all the appliqué pieces in place.

Using the appliqué stitch, begin to attach pieces on the bottom layer (pieces that tuck under). First sew the leaves E, next the large heart-shapes D, and then the small heart-shapes C. Finally, appliqué the circles, and remove all the basting threads.

Behold! The Lancaster Rose!

APPLIQUÉ WITH EMBROIDERY

This is a frequently used combination in quilt-making. You can add embroidery stitches to enhance the design after the appliqué is in place, or you can use decorative stitches to attach the appliqué pieces.

TULIP

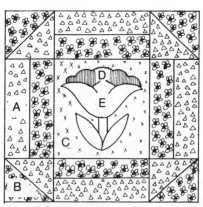

Fig. 59 Tulip
(See also plate 7)

The simple flower design in Fig. 59 is sewed to the foundation square with embroidery floss, using a blanket or buttonhole stitch (instructions follow). The square is then framed with pieced work.

First make templates for the patterns beginning on page 54, and label them. You should also make one additional template—an 8" square C.

Select five fabrics—two solid colors and three prints. The appliqué pieces D and E should be of closely woven fabrics because the edges will not be turned under. Your

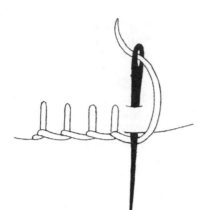

Fig. 60 Blanket stitch

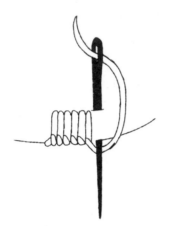

Fig. 61 Buttonhole stitch

Fig. 62 Chain stitch

embroidery stitches will cover and secure the raw edges, but if the fabric tends to fray, eventually the appliqué will pull away from the stitches.

On the *wrong* side of the fabric, trace and cut (adding ½" seam allowances):

    A— 4 of print No. 1
    A— 4 of print No. 2
    B— 4 of print No. 1
    B— 4 of print No. 2
    C— 1 of print No. 3

On the *right* side of the fabric, trace the appliqué pieces and *cut on the pencil lines* (no seam allowance):

    D— 1 of solid color No. 1
    E— 1 of solid color No. 2

With a No. 2 pencil (or yellow pencil on dark fabric), draw the inside design lines. It's all right to use a soft pencil here because your embroidery stitches will cover the lines.

You can draw the lines by eye. Or you can copy the pattern onto tracing paper, then use dressmaker's carbon paper to transfer the design lines to fabric. Go over the lines with a pencil if necessary.

Find the vertical center line of square C by folding the block in half vertically. Finger-press the fold lightly. Then fold appliqué pieces D and E in half vertically and finger-press.

Center the tulip on the square with blossom D tucked under E, along the broken lines on the pattern. Match the vertical fold lines and keep an equal distance from the top and bottom of the square. When you are satisfied with the position, pin and baste the design in place.

Using embroidery stitches

The appliqué pieces are attached to the foundation square with a blanket stitch or a buttonhole stitch. (These are basically the same; the buttonhole version simply has the stitches closer together.)

Use either matching or contrasting embroidery floss. This is packaged with six strands of thread together. Cut off an 18" length of floss and separate two strands from the cut length. (Save the remaining four strands for later use.) Thread an embroidery needle with these two strands of floss, and knot one end.

Use the blanket stitch (Fig. 60) or buttonhole stitch (Fig. 61). To begin, insert the needle into the back of the foundation fabric and bring it out at the edge of the tulip. For the first stitch, hold the thread with your left thumb (right thumb if you are left-handed), and put the needle into the appliqué fabric about ¼" above the point where the thread came out. Bring the needle out at the edge of the appliqué fabric, going over the thread you hold.

Work from left to right, continuing to hold the thread down with each stitch. Take the next stitch about 1/8" away (for the blanket stitch), or closer (for the buttonhole stitch). Hold the thread with your thumb, take each stitch vertically, and bring the needle out over the thread. The spaces between stitches and the depth of the stitches should be uniform.

Continue around the appliqué, covering all the raw edges. Then stitch along the inside design lines. You can continue the same embroidery stitch or switch to the chain stitch (Fig. 62).

To begin the chain stitch, put the needle into the wrong side of the fabric and bring it out at the end of a design line. Make a loop and hold it down with your left thumb (right thumb if you are left-handed). Insert the needle close to where the thread came through the fabric and take a small stitch forward, pulling the needle over the loop you hold. For the next stitch, make a loop, hold it down with your thumb, insert the needle close to where the thread came out (inside the last loop) and take a stitch forward, pulling the needle over the loop you hold. This forms a chain—a nice outline stitch.

Piecing the block

When your embroidery is completed, you are ready to finish the block. Line up all the pieces, following Fig. 59. Join two A pieces at each side to form four large rectangles. Join the B pieces at each corner to form squares. Make a row at the top by sewing the end squares to the rectangle. Repeat to make bottom row.

Sew a rectangle to the right side of the center square, and another to the left side. Finally, stitch the top row and the bottom row to the center section to complete the block. Don't forget to trim the seams and finger-press them as you work.

JEAN'S ROSE

This is a lovely challenge. Jean's Rose (Fig. 63) introduces a new embroidery stitch, provides a review of drafting templates, and gives you an opportunity to build a block with three rows of outside sashing.

Ready with the posterboard and your T-square or triangle! You will use them to draft a square and seven rectangles. Here are the sizes to make:

Square: 9x9"
Rectangles:
  1x9"   1x11"   1x13"   1x15"
  1x10"   1x12"   1x14"

That's a lot of rectangles. Be as accurate as possible in drawing and cutting the templates, and label each one.

On a separate piece of cardboard, transfer the rose design shown on page 60. Slip dressmaker's carbon paper between the book page and cardboard, and trace the design. Remove the carbon paper and cardboard and go over the design with a felt-tip pen to darken the lines.

Now consider the fabrics you will use for the quilt block. You need four different fabrics—two prints and two solid colors. Use a print for the center square and a solid pastel color for the rose appliqué. If you decide on a dark print for the center square, as we did, line the rose appliqué fabric with a non-woven interfacing or with muslin to prevent the dark color from showing through. You can cut the rose and the lining at the same time.

Are you ready for this?

Place the solid color fabric for the rose, right side up, over the cardboard rose design. Anchor the layers with masking tape. With a No. 2 pencil, trace the lines of the rose onto the fabric.

Cut out the rose along the outside lines. Do not add a seam allowance.

On the *wrong* side of the fabric, trace and cut (adding ½" seam allowances):

9" square—1 of print No. 1
1x9"—1 of print No. 2
1x10"—2 of print No. 2
1x11"—1 of print No. 2
1x11"—1 of print No. 1
1x12"—2 of print No. 1
1x13"—1 of print No. 1
1x13"—1 of solid color No. 2
1x14"—2 of solid color No. 2
1x15"—1 of solid color No. 2

print no. 1   *print no. 2*

Fig. 63   Jean's Rose
(See also plate 7)

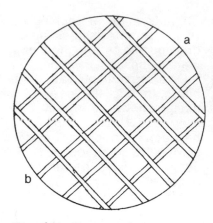

Fig. 64 Center of rose

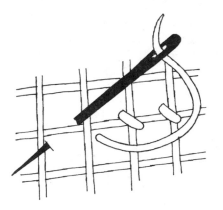

Fig. 65 Couching stitch

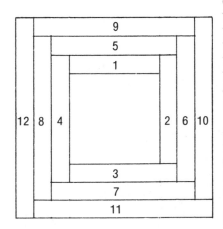

Fig. 66 Guide for piecing
block

Fold the square four times to mark the center (first on the straight grains, then on the diagonals) and finger-press the folds. Center the rose on the square, pin in place and baste.

Embroidering the rose

Use two strands of contrasting embroidery floss to outline the entire rose with the blanket stitch (Fig. 60) or the buttonhole stitch (Fig. 61), attaching it to the foundation square.

Next, embroider the center of the rose. Begin by taking long diagonal stitches across the middle of the circle (Fig. 64). Insert the needle into the back of the work at point (a), and bring the thread through. Cross the circle and take the needle and thread down through the fabric at (b). Continue laying the strands of thread in rows about 3/8″ apart to fill the circle. Repeat the process in the opposite direction.

At this point, the threads are lying on the surface of the rose. To fasten them in place, go back over the surface of the circle, tacking the threads at each intersection with a couching stitch (Fig. 65). For this, bring the needle and thread up below the intersection of two threads. Take the thread diagonally over the intersection. Insert the needle, and bring it out below the next intersection.

When the center is completed, outline the circle with the chain stitch (Fig. 62). Then chain stitch the petal shapes, working from the center of the rose to the outside.

Piecing the block

Now it's time to frame your beautiful rose. Arrange all the fabric pieces in front of you to form the block, using Fig. 66

as a guide. Each strip is numbered to show you the order to follow, and the first four strips are cut from the same print.

1. Add the 1x9″ strip to the top of the center square.

2. Add a 1x10″ strip to the right side.

3. Add a 1x10″ strip to the bottom.

4. Add a 1x11″ strip to the left side.

See how the block is building? Now you begin with strips of another print to form the next square.

5. Add a 1x11″ strip to the top.

6. Add a 1x12″ strip to the right side.

7. Add a 1x12″ strip to the bottom.

8. Add a 1x13″ strip to the left side.

And, now a solid color.

9. Add a 1x13″ strip to the top.

10. Add a 1x14″ strip to the right side.

11. Add a 1x14″ strip to the bottom.

12. Add the 1x15″ strip to the left side.

That completes the block! The technique you have learned for building Jean's Rose is the same one you need to make one of the advanced block designs, the Log Cabin. You are becoming very adept at pieced work.

SUNBONNET SUE AND FARMER BOY

Sunbonnet girls accompanied by their schoolboy companions have been on the American quilting scene for almost a hundred years.

We put these two patterns together since they are often used as a pair, and our blocks are sashed to frame the

Fig. 67   Sunbonnet Sue
(See also plate 10)

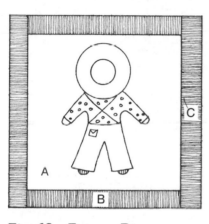

Fig. 68   Farmer Boy
(See also plate 10)

designs. Sunbonnet Sue (Fig. 67) and Farmer Boy (Fig. 68) let you be creative, especially with embroidery stitches. We give you the basic pattern outlines, and you can add the extras. Our sample blocks on plate 10 show Sue carrying a picnic basket and Farmer Boy holding a colorful balloon. There is a bias binding trim on Sue's sunbonnet.

First, make templates from the patterns beginning on page 58. Copy the inside design lines as you did for Jean's Rose, and make a separate template for Sue's arm and hand.

Draw three other templates—a 12″ square A for the foundation pieces and two rectangles, B (1½x12″) and C (1½x15″) for the sashing. Be sure to make the corners perfectly square.

Select fabrics for each block. Choose a solid color for the foundation square and another solid color for the sashing. Repeat the sashing color in some of the appliqué pieces.

For each block, trace on the *wrong* side of the fabric, and cut (adding ½″ seam allowances):

    A—1 of solid color No. 1
    B—2 of solid color No. 2
    C—2 of solid color No. 2

Center the large template (Sunbonnet Sue or Farmer Boy) on square A and trace around it with a No. 5H or 6H pencil. This will guide you in placing the appliqué pieces later. Now cut the template apart along the solid lines, and label each piece. (The broken lines indicate embroidery or trim lines.)

On the *right* side of the fabric, trace and cut (adding ½″ seam allowances):

    All appliqué pieces in
    selected fabrics.

Before you prepare the appliqué pieces, first determine how they will be arranged. Wherever two pieces come together, one should overlap the other. For example, Sue's sunbonnet overlaps the top of her dress, so the seam allowance on the dress is tucked under the bonnet.

Prepare the appliqué pieces by stay-stitching around each one just outside the pencil lines. Slash where necessary, and turn the edges neatly to the wrong side. *Note:* Do not turn under any edge that tucks under another appliqué piece.

Baste along the turned edges, trim any excess fabric and press with an iron.

Position the pieces for one design on a foundation square. Pin and baste in place, then attach the pieces with the appliqué stitch (Fig. 56). Appliqué Sue's arm and hand on top of her dress.

Use fabric or bias binding strips for Farmer Boy's overall straps, or embroider them later. Use a chain stitch (Fig. 62) to add details such as the boy's pocket and crown of his hat.

Embellish blocks to your heart's content. Use ribbon, lace, rickrack or embroidery stitches. Add background touches, such as birds, flowers, clouds and trees. You can see why the blocks have remained popular for so many years—they're such fun for quilters!

Finally, add sashing pieces B to the top and bottom of square A. Then add sashing pieces C to the sides.

These two designs make attractive pillow tops (children love them), or you can set the blocks in your sampler quilt. But beware—the young members of your family may soon request whole quilts of Sunbonnet Sue and Farmer Boy.

APPLIQUÉ WITH PIECED WORK

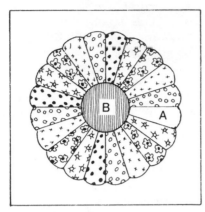

Fig. 69   Dresden Plate

(See also plate 10)

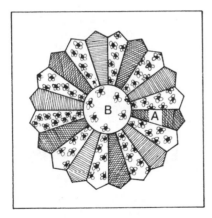

Fig. 70   Aster

(See also plate 10)

For our first design, the appliqué is pieced, then it is sewed in place. For another design, the block itself is completely pieced, then the appliqué is added.

DRESDEN PLATE AND ASTER

According to legend, one day a quilter took one of her prized Dresden plates, turned it upside down on a piece of paper and traced around it. Then she divided the circle as if it were a pie, made a small center circle, and the pattern for Dresden Plate (Fig. 69) was born. With a slight variation, using pointed petals instead of rounded ones, the design becomes the Aster (Fig. 70). For now, we will concentrate on the Dresden Plate.

There are 20 petals in the design. Choose a solid color for the foundation block, then use any combination of fabrics you like for the petals. Each petal may be different, or you could use five fabrics, repeating each one four times—those are just two possibilities.

First, make two templates from the patterns on page 54. Then find your 15″ square template to use for the foundation square.

On the *wrong* side of the fabric, trace and cut (adding ½″ seam allowances):

   15″ square—1 of solid color

   A—20 of selected fabrics

On the *right* side of the fabric, trace and cut (adding ½″ seam allowances):

   B—1 of solid color

Piecing the plate

Arrange the petals A in a circle on the foundation block to find a color grouping that pleases you. Pick up two adjoining petals and stitch them together along the pencil lines, but stop the stitching exactly where the curve begins. The loose edges will be folded under.

When all 20 petals are pieced together, turn the outside curved edges to the wrong side. You have two choices now—remember?

You can: (1) Put a row of stitches just outside the pencil lines, slash the seam allowances, turn the raw edges to the wrong side, baste along the edges as you did with the Heart appliqué, trim the excess fabric and press. Or you can: (2) Turn the plate face down on the ironing board, put the petal template on each petal and iron the curve over the template. (But please don't burn your fingers!) Then baste the edges and trim.

Leave the inner circle of the petals flat. Those raw edges will be covered later.

Appliquéing the plate

Fold the foundation square four times to find the center (first on the grain lines and then on the diagonals) and finger-press. Position the Dresden Plate in the center of the foundation block and baste it in place. Attach the design with the appliqué stitch (Fig. 56).

Take circle B, turn the raw edge to the wrong side as you did for the petal curves, center it over the raw edges of the petals and appliqué it in place.

There! A beautiful, unbreakable Dresden Plate.

Why not try the Aster next?

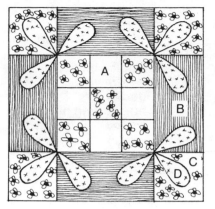

Fig. 71   Honey Bee
(See also plate 7)

HONEY BEE

This nature-inspired design (Fig. 71) also is known as Bit of Spring. It differs from some of the previous designs in that the block must be completely pieced before the appliqué can be added.

The block is very effective when brown and yellow are used as the predominant colors to heighten the effect of honey bees, but any color combination can be used.

Make the four templates from patterns on page 57 and label them. Select four fabrics—two solid colors and two prints. On the *wrong* side of the fabric, trace and cut (adding ½″ seam allowances):

A—4 of solid color No. 1
A—5 of print No. 1
B—4 of solid color No. 2
C—4 of print No. 1

On the *right* side of the fabric, trace and cut (adding ½″ seam allowances):

D — 12 of print No. 2

Arrange the pieces for the block in front of you. To make the center square, join small squares A to form three rows, then sew the rows together.

To make the top row of the block, add a corner square C to each end of a rectangle B. Repeat to make the bottom row.

Sew a rectangle B to each side of the nine-patch center square. Finally, stitch the top and bottom rows to the center section.

To prepare the bee designs, stay-stitch just outside the pencil lines, slash the seam allowances, turn and baste raw edges to the wrong side, trim excess fabric, and press with an iron.

Position the bee appliqué pieces. Use matching thread to sew them to the block with the appliqué stitch (Fig. 56).

APPLIQUÉ WITH PAPER

For some quilt blocks where many small pieces must fit together, you can make the job easier by shaping the fabric over paper templates. After the pieces are sewed together, you remove (or pop) the papers. The English are credited with developing this method.

GRANDMOTHER'S FLOWER GARDEN

This pattern was used by Persian and Indian quilters for centuries before the Crusaders took it back to Europe. Today, if you asked 50 quilters to name their favorite designs, Grandmother's Flower Garden (Fig. 72) would probably rank high on the list. Because it's such a popular pattern, we chose it for our Beginner's Sampler Quilt, and we use it as an appliqué.

The basic unit in this design is a hexagon measuring 1½″ on each edge. Think about sewing these little pieces together. "Impossible," you say. Not at all. In fact, we're sure you will thoroughly enjoy making this block. It's easy, and the paper templates are the secret.

**Many templates,
three fabrics**

Make one template of the hexagon pattern on page 54. (Plastic is a good choice for this because it will be traced

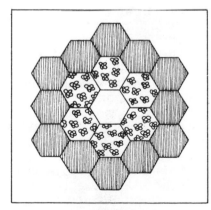

Fig. 72   Grandmother's Flower Garden
(See also plate 10)

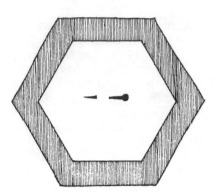

Fig. 73 Using template to cut fabric

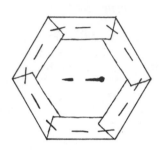

Fig. 74 Basting fabric over template

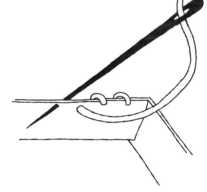

Fig. 75 Whipping stitch

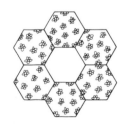

Fig. 76 Center of design

many times.) Then trace the template, not on fabric, but on paper. Use old envelopes, magazine pages, stationery or any firm paper. Make 19 paper hexagons, and cut them out exactly on the pencil lines. Then find your 15″ square template to use for the foundation square. (You made it in Chapter 1 for the String block.)

Choose three fabrics—two solids and one print. Use your 15″-square template to trace and cut (adding ½″ seam allowances) one square of solid color No. 1; trace on the *wrong* side of the fabric.

Cutting and joining hexagons

Now for the fun of putting the design together. First, place a paper pattern on the *wrong* side of solid color No. 1. This will be the center of the design. Pin the paper to the fabric with the top and bottom edges on the grain lines. By eye, gauge a ½″ seam allowance and cut the fabric (Fig. 73). Turn the raw edges down over the paper and baste (Fig. 74).

Follow the same steps to cut and shape six hexagons of the print fabric for the middle ring. Then cut 12 hexagons of solid color No. 2 for the outside ring.

Arrange the basted hexagons in front of you, right side up, according to Fig. 72. With the paper still inside, you are ready to sew the hexagons together—by hand.

Place the center hexagon and one from the middle ring, right sides together, along a straight edge. Use a whipping stitch (Fig. 75) to join them. Slant your needle and catch only a few threads at the edge

of each piece to whip them together. Keep your stitches small and close together, and try not to catch the paper. If you do catch a bit of paper occasionally, however, don't worry about it.

Continue adding hexagons around the ring. First sew each hexagon to the center one, and then to an adjoining piece. When the six hexagons are attached to the center and form a ring, you have a rosette (Fig. 76).

Complete the mosaic shape by adding the outside ring of hexagons. Join each one first to the middle ring, and then to an adjoining hexagon. Pay particular attention to fitting the shapes together neatly.

Popping the papers

The design is finished, but what about all that paper? When our foremothers made this quilt design, they left the paper inside the fabric to add warmth to the quilt. Many of those paper patterns were cut out of letters from home and have provided an excellent means of dating old quilts. However, we are going to remove the paper. Here's how:

After the hexagons are sewed together, snip the basting stitches around the center hexagon and pull them out. As you do this, the paper actually pops out! Remove the bastings from the middle ring and pop the papers.

Before you pop the papers of the outside hexagons, press the completed design with an iron. This molds the fabric and helps keep the outside lines sharp. It is best to leave the papers in this ring until you are actually ready to appliqué the design to the foundation fabric. At that point, remove the bastings, pop the papers and baste the edges to hold them in place.

Appliquéing the garden

Fold the foundation square four times to find the exact center (first on the grain lines, then on the diagonals) and finger-press the folds. Find the center of the middle hexagon. Insert a pin at this point in the hexagon, taking the same pin through the center of the foundation square. (Be sure the appliqué is lined up evenly along the sides of the foundation square.) Anchor the pin. Use more pins to hold the design in place, then baste.

With the appliqué stitch and matching thread, attach the Flower Garden, completing the quilt block.

Congratulations! You have mastered the technique of English piecing as well as appliqué. You have also completed all the blocks in the beginner's section of this book, and you are very close to assembling those blocks for your very own Beginner's Sampler Quilt.

Patterns

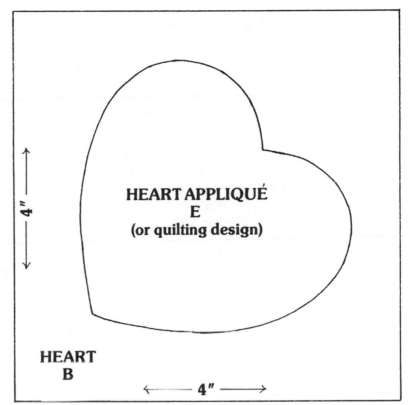

4"

HEART APPLIQUÉ
E
(or quilting design)

HEART
B

← 4" →

4"

HEART
A

← 7" →

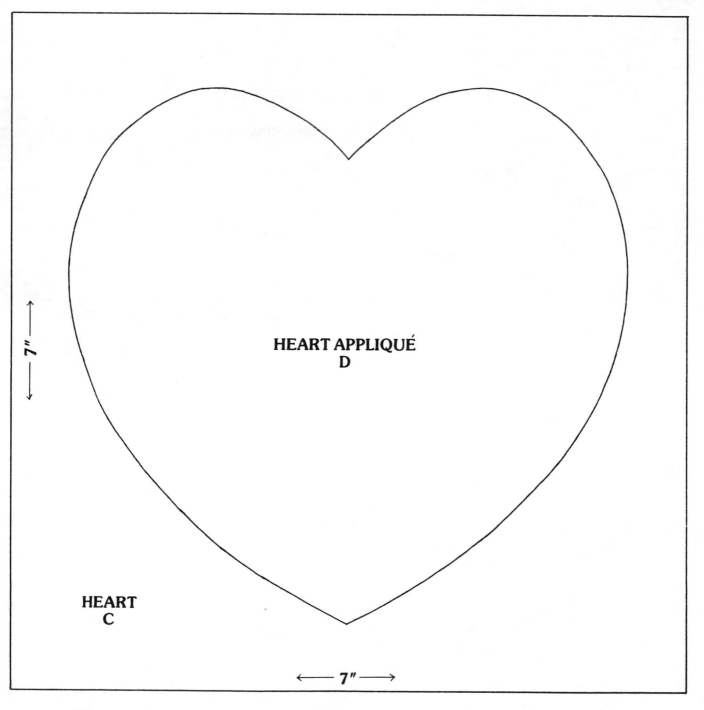

7"

**HEART APPLIQUÉ
D**

**HEART
C**

7"

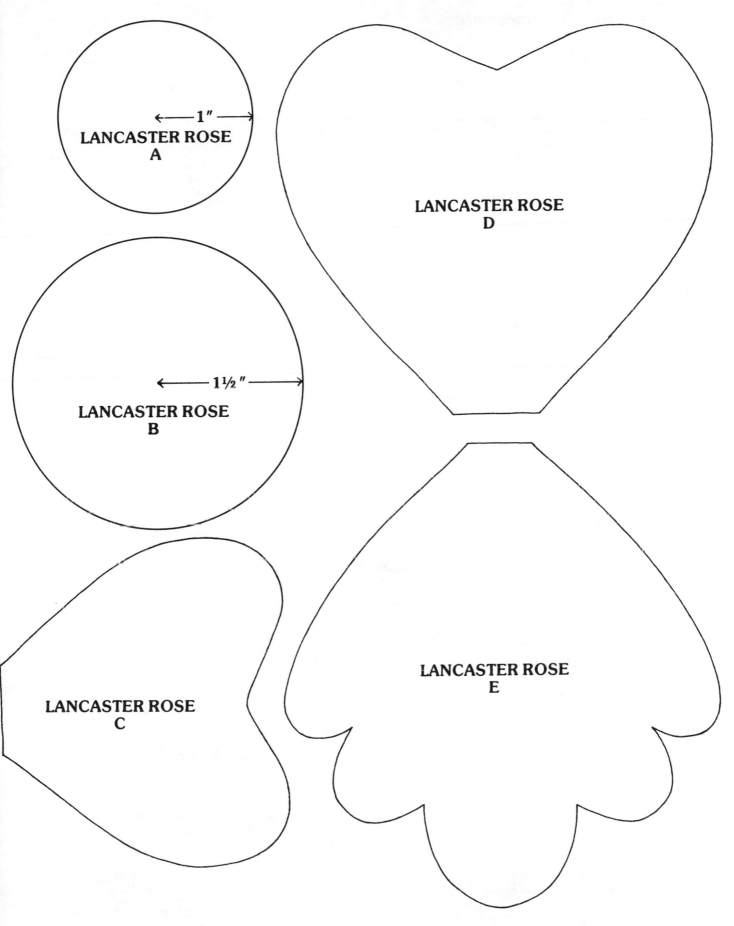

LANCASTER ROSE
A

LANCASTER ROSE
D

LANCASTER ROSE
B

LANCASTER ROSE
C

LANCASTER ROSE
E

53

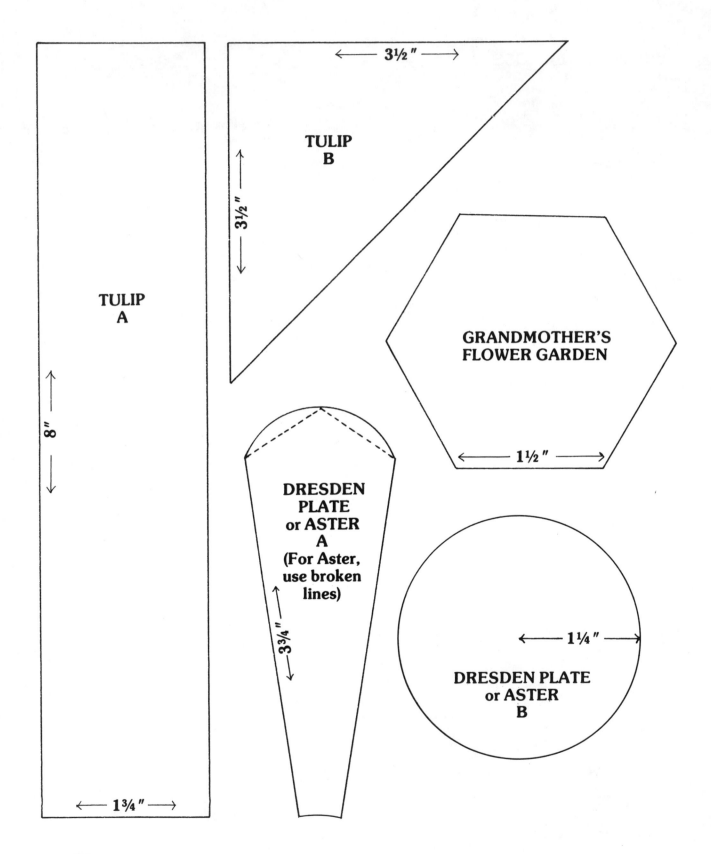

TULIP
A

8"

1¾"

3½"

TULIP
B

3½"

GRANDMOTHER'S
FLOWER GARDEN

1½"

DRESDEN
PLATE
or ASTER
A
(For Aster,
use broken
lines)

3¾"

DRESDEN PLATE
or ASTER
B

1¼"

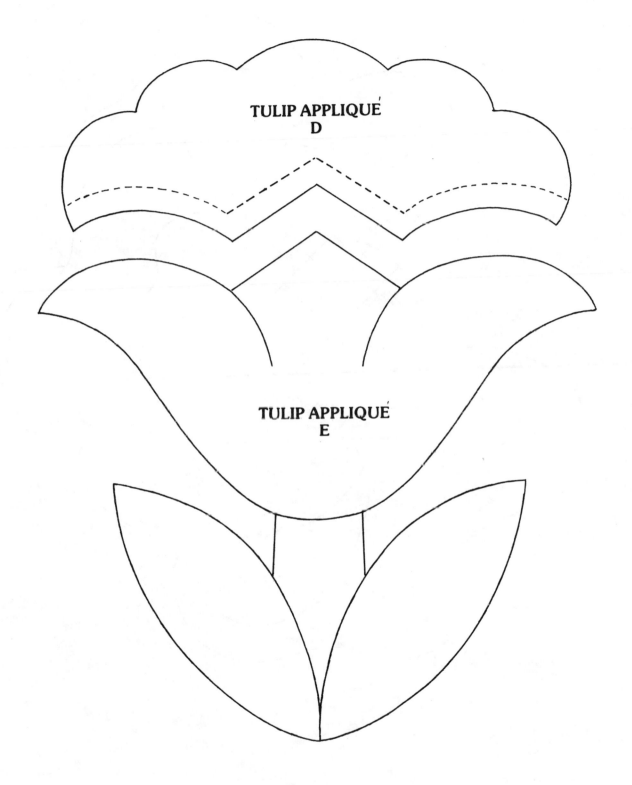

**TULIP APPLIQUÉ
D**

**TULIP APPLIQUÉ
E**

JEAN'S ROSE

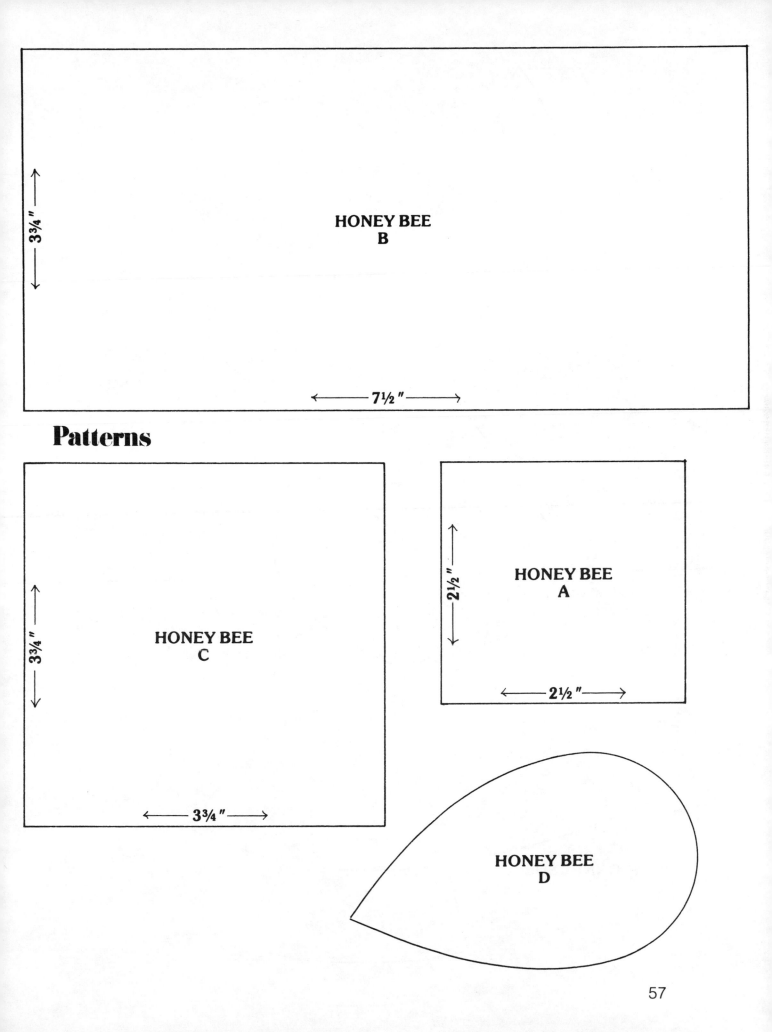

**HONEY BEE
B**

↕ 3¾ "

← 7½ " →

Patterns

**HONEY BEE
C**

↕ 3¾ "

← 3¾ " →

**HONEY BEE
A**

↕ 2½ "

← 2½ " →

**HONEY BEE
D**

SUNBONNET SUE

58

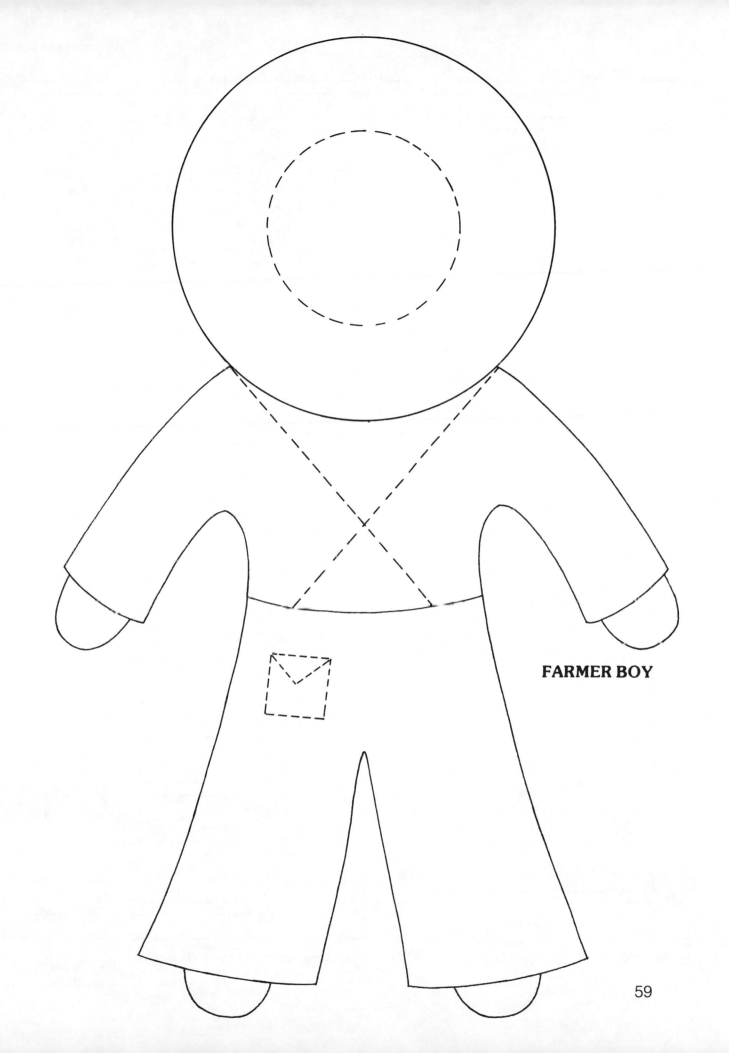

FARMER BOY

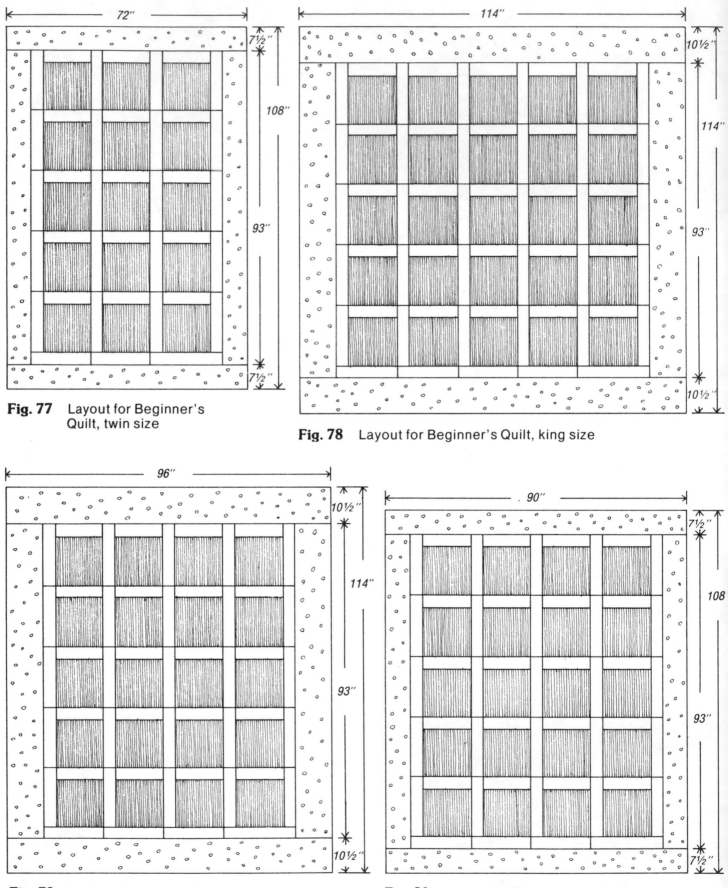

Fig. 77   Layout for Beginner's
Quilt, twin size

Fig. 78   Layout for Beginner's Quilt, king size

Fig. 79   Layout for Beginner's Quilt, queen size

Fig. 80   Layout for Beginner's Quilt, full size

6 Assemble your quilt— and quilt it

If you have stayed with us this far, you are the proud maker of more than 20 quilt blocks. It's time to chose the ones you will set in your quilt.

Check the exact number of blocks you need for the size quilt you plan to make (Figs. 77-80). For most sizes, you will have to eliminate a few blocks, but these can be turned into pillow tops or tote bags. (Directions for making a tote are in Chapter 7).

For the king-size quilt, you will have to add a few more blocks. Will you make another Grandmother's Flower Garden? Or a simple Shoofly? Maybe you'll want to add a sashed block so that you can quilt the Single Feathered Plate design as you did for your quilted pillow in Chapter 4. Pick your favorite quilt block patterns and use different fabric combinations this time.

PREPARING ROWS AND BORDER

After you have chosen the blocks for your quilt, you must decide on how to arrange them.

Place the blocks on the floor of your living room or some other large area. Study them. Move the blocks around. Put the least interesting designs on the sides and the ones you like best in the middle where you will see them on top of the bed. Turn the blocks sideways or upside down if they look better in the overall layout. (In our Beginner's Sampler Quilt, we turned the String block around.)

Walk away from the arrangement and then come back to it. Is it still as attractive as you first thought it was? Try to balance the colors. Continue looking at the arrangement. Narrow your eyes and look at the quilt pieces. If a particular color or design seems to dominate the arrangement, move it to another location.

When you are totally satisfied with the choice and placement of the blocks, make a diagram of the layout and write the name of each block in the corresponding square.

Extra quilting lines

Take another look at the blocks to see if you want to add lines or designs for extra quilting. You should have all lines to be quilted penciled before you put the quilt layers together. It is almost impossible to trace patterns accurately after the batting is in place.

Any open space on a solid color is an invitation to do a little fancy quilting. (Since your work won't show up on prints, there's not much use in putting extra stitches there.) Mark light-colored fabrics with a sharp No. 5H or 6H pencil, and mark dark fabrics with a sharp yellow pencil.

Here are two quilting ideas to consider. On the Grandmother's Flower Garden block, use your hexagon template and trace an outside ring of hexagons. On the Dresden Plate block, use a ruler and extend the seam lines between the petals to the outside edges of the block.

We also offer three small quilting patterns on page 71. Transfer the designs according to the fabric you are using.

For light-colored fabric that you can see through, make a

cardboard template of the design. Use dressmaker's carbon to trace the design from this book onto the cardboard, then go over the lines with a felt-tip pen. To transfer the design to fabric, tape the template under the fabric and trace the design onto the right side with a No. 5H or 6H pencil.

For dark-colored fabric that you can't see through, skip the cardboard template and use tracing paper. First put the tracing paper over the design in this book and trace the lines. Then position the tracing-paper drawing on top of the fabric (right side up), slip white carbon paper under the tracing paper, and anchor the layers with masking tape or pins.

Work on a hard surface, and retrace the design with a No. 2 pencil. Bear down so you can see the carbon lines on the fabric. Remove the paper. If necessary, go over the lines lightly with a yellow pencil.

Adding the sashing

The next step is to sew sashing pieces to the blocks, and you've already had some experience with this. You probably purchased the sashing fabric earlier (yardage is given in Chapter 1).

First, draw templates to make the job of cutting the pieces easier. You need three rectangles of posterboard—3x15", 3x18" and 3x21". Use these to trace the number of fabric pieces for your quilt size (see chart below left). Add ½" seam allowances as you cut the fabric.

Making the rows

Line up the blocks you have chosen for Row 1, the top row of your quilt. Arrange the sashing along the top and sides of the blocks, following Fig. 81, and join the pieces in this order:

1. Sew a 3x15" strip of

Number of sashing pieces needed				
Sizes	twin	full (double)	queen	king
3x15"*	15	20	20	25
3x18"*	22	28	28	34
3x21"*	1	1	1	1
* Add ½" seam allowances when cutting				

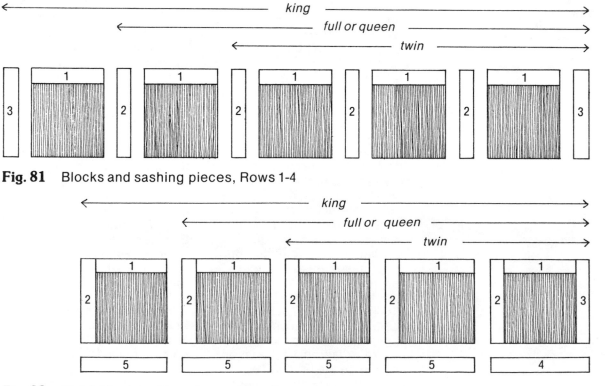

Fig. 81 Blocks and sashing pieces, Rows 1-4

Fig. 82 Blocks and sashing pieces, Row 5

sashing to the top of each block.

2. Sew a 3x18" strip of sashing between the blocks.

3. Sew a 3x18" strip of sashing at each end of the row. This completes Row 1.

4. Repeat Steps 1-3 to complete Rows 2, 3 and 4.

Now, line up the blocks for Row 5, the bottom row. Arrange the sashing following Fig. 82 and join the pieces in this order:

1. Sew a 3x15" strip of sashing to the top of each block.

2. Sew a 3x18" strip of sashing to the left side of each block.

3. Sew an extra 3x18" strip of sashing to the block at the extreme right.

4. Sew a 3x21" strip of sashing to the bottom of the block at the extreme right.

5. Sew a 3x18" strip of sashing to the bottom of all other blocks.

6. Join the blocks to make Row 5.

Measure your bed

Beds do vary in height, and your mattress may even differ a bit from the standard size. Now is the time to check your bed to be sure the quilt will fit over it as you wish. You can alter dimensions easily by adding inches to, or subtracting inches from, the outside borders that are not yet cut.

The side borders should always be the same width, but the top and bottom borders can be different.

Our layout charts (Figs. 77-80) give the overall dimensions of each quilt size, and the chart in the next column lists standard mattress sizes.

For example, let's compare a full-size bed with a full-size quilt (Fig. 80). A standard full-size mattress is 54" across, and the quilt is 90" across.

Standard mattress sizes	
twin	39x75"
full	54x75"
queen	60x80"
king	76x80"

That leaves 36" extra, or 18" of overhang on each side of the bed. Now look at the length. The full-size mattress is 75" long; the quilt is 108" long. That leaves 33" to cover the pillows at the top and to provide overhang at the foot. If you want to change the overall size of the quilt, note the changes for the border pieces on the layout for your quilt size.

Usually, you don't want the quilt to touch the floor. A dust ruffle in a coordinating color can be used to fill in the space between the quilt and the floor.

Measuring the border pieces

Find the print you purchased for the border (yardage given in Chapter 1). Then use the chart below to find the dimensions you need for your quilt size. *Note:* If you have altered the dimensions, be sure to change them on the chart below, too, adding ½" seam allowances on all sides.

The top and bottom border pieces run across the full width of the quilt. The side pieces run between the top and bottom borders.

It isn't practical to make a template for such long lengths, so you have to measure differently.

First, measure along the selvage edge to find the length you need (91" for the top border of the full-size quilt), and mark it with a pin or snip of the shears. Next, go back and measure the width from the selvage (8½" for the full-size quilt). At that point, make a small cut in the fabric along a lengthwise thread. Then tear the fabric up to the length you need, and cut or tear across the width.

Mark and tear a second strip for the bottom edge. Then mark and tear two strips for the sides.

Note: You may have to piece some border strips. The seams won't be noticable in the finished quilt, especially if you're using a printed fabric.

Press the border strips before you add them to the quilt. Tearing sometimes pulls the fabric out of line, but pressing should restore it.

Border dimensions*		twin	full	queen	king
For top and bottom; cut 2		8½x73"	8½x91"	11½x97"	11½x115"
For sides; cut 2		8½x94"	8½x94"	1½x94"	11½x94"
*Includes ½" seam allowances					

63

TWO METHODS OF QUILTING

You have five rows of blocks with sashing, four pieces of border and one burning question— "How do I quilt this thing?" We offer two choices.

You can add batting and backing fabric to the rows of blocks, and quilt the single rows before they are sewed together. Or you can com-

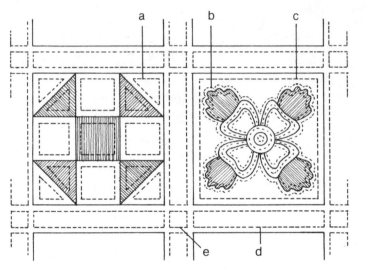

Fig. 83 Guide for quilting stitches

plete the quilt top, add batting and backing, and use a hoop to quilt the larger unit.

Quilting in rows lets you hold the layers in your hands and manipulate them easily. There is less bulk to handle than when working with the whole quilt, and you may find this an advantage if your space is limited.

A hoop, on the other hand, holds the layers taut, as does a large quilting frame. This keeps your quilting uniform.

With either method, your work is portable.

We give you directions for these two quilting methods beginning on the next page, so that you can decide which to use. The general quilting

tips that follow apply to both methods.

General quilting tips

• *Use quilting needles* (Betweens size 7 or 8).
• *Use quilting thread* (see "Quilting thread," page 13). Since your quilt fabrics are in a variety of colors, you may choose to use quilting thread to match each color. This helps keep your stitches inconspicuous. However, if you like to see a well-defined pattern on the underside of the quilt, don't hesitate to use the same color of thread for all the quilting. If your stitches are uniform, they will be attractive. An occasional stitch might fail to measure up to standard, but it will not be noticed on such a wide expanse of fabric.
• *Work from the center to the outside,* and always start work where you left off. Begin quilting at the center, then quilt the surrounding area, and so on. Gradually work outward in all directions. Each quilting stitch pushes the batting outward, and if you do not work in this manner, you will discover that strange lumps develop in your quilt.
• *Quilt ¼" away from seam lines.* Otherwise, you will encounter extra fabric (and this might cause you do swear off quilting forever).
• *Use quilting stitches* to define patterns (Fig. 83). On pieced-work blocks, quilt along both sides of the seam lines (a). On appliqué blocks, quilt around the appliqué shapes (b). Also, quilt inside the shapes as you wish. (We usually omit inside quilting stitches when the appliqué is applied with embroidery stitches.) Quilt around each block inside the seam line (c).

On the sashing strips, quilt rectangles (d) to line up with the blocks, and quilt squares

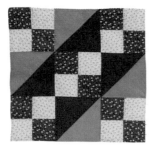

Quilt top using a single design (Jacob's Ladder), set without sashing. By Jessie MacDonald.

Plate 9

Beginner's blocks

Grandmother's Flower Garden

Sunbonnet Sue

Farmer Boy

Dresden Plate

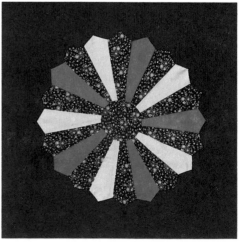

Aster

Plate 10

Advanced blocks

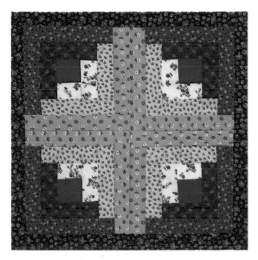

Log Cabin

Ocean Waves

Mexican Star

54-40 or Fight

Plate 11

Plate 12

Sampler quilt with 12 patchwork
blocks, combining beginner's
and advanced designs.
By Elinor Shoop.

Tote bags display single patchwork blocks. You'll find
directions for making totes in Chapter 7.

Plate 13

Advanced blocks

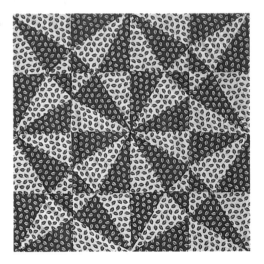

Crossed Canoes

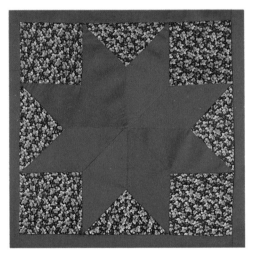

Eight-Pointed Star

Virginia Star

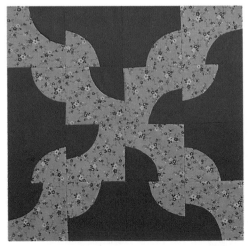

Plate 14

Drunkard's Path

Advanced blocks

Grandmother's Fan

Hands All Around

Baby Blocks

Clamshell

Plate 15

Plate 16

Advanced Sampler Quilt with
12 patchwork blocks.
By Jessie MacDonald.

(e) at the corners of the blocks.

• *Try to gauge the quilting lines* with your eye. If you feel the need of a guide, however, you can draw quilting lines. Use a No. 5H or 6H pencil on light colors, and a yellow pencil (or even a sliver of soap) on dark fabrics. These marks disappear as you quilt.

Backing and batting

Before you begin quilting, you will have to put your finished rows or quilt top over batting and a backing fabric to make the sandwich.

The quilt backing fabric seldom shows, so it is one place where you can use a bargain. Perhaps you can find a good quality fabric that has been reduced or specially priced.

Of course, the backing should blend with the fabrics in the quilt top. It can be a print or solid color, though a print does help hide the seams. It can be a cotton or cotton blend, but it should wear well and be easy to quilt. (Do not use sheeting. This is too tightly woven and is difficult to quilt.)

Batting is sold in rolls of various sizes, including 45x60", 72x90", 81x96" and 90x108". You may even find larger sizes.

Buy bonded polyester batting. The bonded face makes it easier to handle and prevents the batting from working its way (bleeding) through the quilt top and pilling on the quilt surface.

The yardage you need for backing fabric and batting will depend on the method you choose for quilting. So, *read the rest of this chapter to help you decide on the quilting method.* Then buy materials according to the chart below.

If you quilt in single rows

With this first method, you quilt one row or strip at a time. Work in this order:

1. *Stack the layers.* Measure across a row of blocks, then cut or tear a piece of backing fabric the same length as the row, but 1" wider (20" wide for Rows 1-4). Lay the backing, right side down, on the floor. Cut a piece of batting the same size as the row and center it on top of the backing. Then put the first quilt row (Row 1 of your blocks) on top of the batting, right side up. Pin the three layers together to hold them in place. *Note:* Backing fabric extends ½" beyond the blocks at both top and bottom of the row.

2. *Baste the layers together,* following Fig. 84. Use white mercerized cotton thread and begin in the middle block of the row. Baste from the center to the outside of the block, first along the straight grains (Lines 1-2-3-4), then along the diagonals (Lines 5-6-7-8). Baste around the block directly on top of the

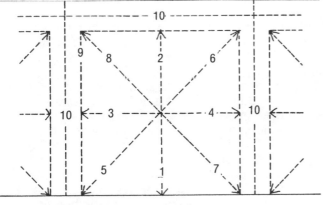

Fig. 84 Guide for basting layers when you quilt single rows

Backing and batting needed				
	twin	**full**	**queen**	**king**
If you quilt in single rows: Backing fabric, 45" wide	8 yd.	10 yd.	11 yd.	12 yd.
Batting	2 pkg. (72x90")	2 pkg. (72x90")	2 pkg. (81x96")	2 pkg. (90x108")
If you quilt with a hoop: Backing fabric, 45" wide	6½ yd.	7¾ yd.	8¼ yd.	11 yd.
Batting	1 pkg. (90x108")	1 pkg. (90x108")	1 pkg. (81x96") 1 pkg. (72x90")	1 pkg. (90x108") 1 pkg. (72x90")

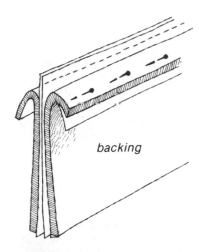

Fig. 85 Joining quilted rows

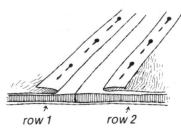

row 1   row 2

Fig. 86 Trimming batting

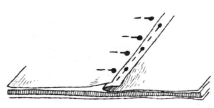

Fig. 87 Backing in place for final quilting

Fig. 88 Pinning backing fabric

seam line (Line 9).

Repeat, basting the lines on all other blocks, working away from the center block.

Finally, baste down the center of each sashing piece (Lines numbered 10). When you finish, you have a neat package to handle.

3. *Begin quilting in the center* of the row, following the guides under "General quilting tips," page 64. *Note:* When you are quilting a single row, you must stop about 1" from all raw edges. After the row is stitched to an adjoining row or border piece, you can complete the quilting lines.

When Row 1 is quilted, pull out your basting threads. Admire your work! See how the designs stand out when they are quilted.

Repeat the steps to quilt Row 2.

4. *Sew the quilted rows together.* Take Rows 1 and 2, and place them right sides together (see Fig. 85). Pin along the edges, matching the pencil lines. (Pin loose edges of batting and backing fabric out of the way.) Stitch the two rows together, making sure all intersections of seams meet exactly. Trim the seam allowance to just under ¼", and finger-press to one side.

Lay the joined rows flat on a table, with the blocks facing down. Unpin the batting, but keep backing fabric pinned out of the way.

Smooth the loose edge of Row 1 batting into place, letting it extend ½" beyond the seam you just stitched. Trim if necessary. (Be careful. It is very easy to cut the quilt at this crucial point.)

Smooth Row 2 batting into place, and trim so that it just meets (butts against) Row 1 batting (Fig. 86).

Next, unpin Row 1 backing fabric and smooth it over the

batting. Pin or baste to secure (Fig. 87). Finish quilting the lines on Row 1, then trim the backing fabric, leaving only ¼" seam allowance beyond the quilting stitches.

Unpin Row 2 backing and smooth out flat; pin or baste to secure. Finish quilting along the edge of Row 2.

Let Row 2 backing overlap Row 1. Turn the raw edge under ½" and sew in place (Fig. 88). Use the appliqué stitch (Fig. 56) for a secure seam.

Quilt Row 3, then stitch it to Row 2, following the directions above. Continue until you have quilted and joined all five rows of the quilt. *Note:* Backing strip for Row 5 should be 23" wide—1" wider than the row. (Row 5 is wider than the other rows because it has an extra width of sashing.)

When all the rows are joined, trim the excess backing fabric from the top and bottom edges so that all layers are the same size.

5. *Add the borders.* If you are tired of quilting, you can omit it on the borders. However, you may want to quilt the borders, too. If so, now is the time to mark the quilting lines. You may use a special design or simply draw straight lines that run parallel to the edge of the border. (Refer to "Extra quilting lines," page 61.)

To prepare the border sections, cut or tear a piece of backing fabric the same length as each border piece, and ½" wider.

Lay one backing strip on the floor, right side down. Add a layer of batting cut the same size as the border, then add the matching border piece, right side up. Have the layers even along one edge, and baste them together. (The extra ½" on the backing fabric will form an overlap when the

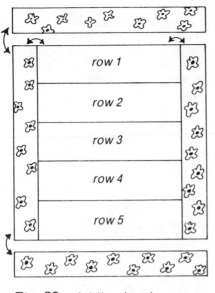

Fig. 89 Adding border sections

border is stitched to the center of the quilt.)

Repeat the process to stack and baste the three other border sections.

Do any quilting you wish.

Next, sew the borders to the center section, beginning with the side borders (Fig. 89). Position each border section so that the extra ½" is next to the center of the quilt. Follow the same procedure you used for sewing the rows together in Step 4.

In summary: Stitch the border piece to the top layer of the center section, trim the batting and smooth the backing fabric into place. Finish any quilting on the blocks and border, let the backing on the border section overlap the center section, and hand-stitch the overlap in place.

Complete both side borders, then add the top and bottom border sections.

6. *Finish the edges.* This last step is described later on page 69.

If you quilt with a hoop

For this second method of quilting, you work with the whole quilt as a unit, and the hoop keeps the layers from shifting. The hoop rests easily on a table or chair as you work, and you can transport it with little difficulty. When you are not quilting, both the hoop and quilt fit into a large plastic bag (blanket- size) for storage.

We recommend a round wooden quilt hoop or rug hoop, 23" in diameter. Some

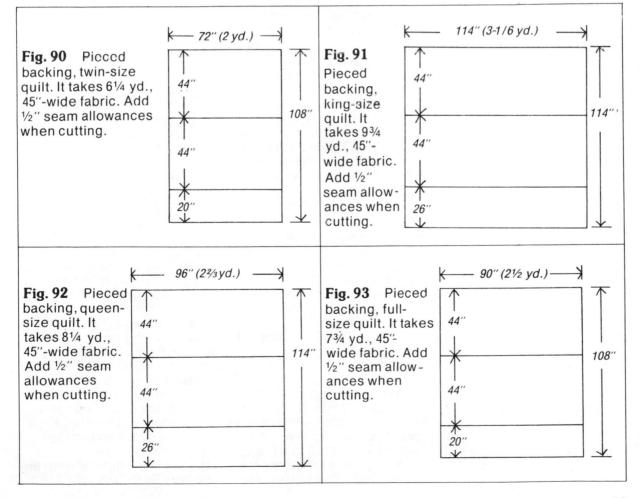

Fig. 90 Pieced backing, twin-size quilt. It takes 6¼ yd., 45"-wide fabric. Add ½" seam allowances when cutting.

Fig. 91 Pieced backing, king-size quilt. It takes 9¾ yd., 45"-wide fabric. Add ½" seam allow- ances when cutting.

Fig. 92 Pieced backing, queen-size quilt. It takes 8¼ yd., 45"-wide fabric. Add ½" seam allowances when cutting.

Fig. 93 Pieced backing, full-size quilt. It takes 7¾ yd., 45"- wide fabric. Add ½" seam allow- ances when cutting.

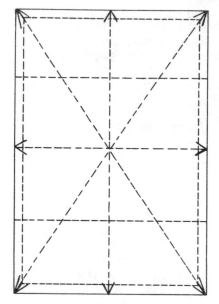

Fig. 94 Guide for basting layers when quilt top is completed and you quilt with a hoop

people find a 17½x27" oval hoop easier to handle, but the oval does not hold fabric quite so taut.

To quilt with a hoop, follow these steps:

1. *Join the rows of blocks.* After you stitch the sashing pieces to the blocks to form rows (Figs. 81 and 82), stitch all the rows together. (Pin-baste, stitch, trim and press). Next, add the border pieces, first the sides, and then the top and bottom. There! You have a quilt top.

2. *Prepare the backing fabric.* Piece lengths of backing fabric together to make one large section the same size as your quilt top. Follow the diagram for your quilt size (Figs. 90-93).

Note: Diagrams show finished sizes, using 45"-wide fabric. Be sure to measure the width of your fabric and to allow ½" seam allowances.

Press the completed backing section and the quilt top with an iron.

3. *Stack the layers.* Place the backing, right side down, on a large rug. Pin the backing to the rug (T-pins are excellent for this). Place pins about 3" apart across the top, then pin along the bottom in the same way, pulling the fabric taut with each insertion of a pin. Pin the sides last, pulling the fabric taut. When your pinning is complete, there should not be a wrinkle.

Now, stand up, stretch your cramped back and massage your pink knees.

Open the batting, roll it out and spread it evenly over the backing. For the twin and full-size quilts, one sheet of batting is large enough. For the queen and king sizes, however, you probably will have to piece the batting. When piecing, have the batting edges just meet (butt together); they should not overlap. Use large,

loose stitches through the batting to hold the edges together. Then trim, so the batting is the same size as the backing.

When the batting is in place, remove every other pin from the backing, but see that the backing remains taut. Then replace the pins, this time going through the batting and back into the rug.

Finally, place the quilt top over the batting, right side up, and pin the three layers together. Keep them taut by pinning through to the rug.

4. *Baste the layers together.* You probably expected this next step. If you want to move the quilt off the floor so that you can sit to baste, repin the layers. Lift each pin and reinsert it to hold the layers together. In addition, pin the corners of each block of the quilt top. Then you can take the quilt to a large table to work.

Of course, you can baste the quilt right on the floor. (Try not to catch the rug in your stitches.) Take off your shoes and start at the center. It will take you about an hour and a half.

Instead of threading your needle with a long piece of thread that will eventually tangle or knot, just thread a long darning needle to the end of the spool of mercerized white cotton thread, and sew all the way from the center to an edge before you cut the thread.

Baste from the center along the straight grain to the top and bottom edges, then to each side (Fig. 94).

Baste from the center to each corner on a diagonal line. Baste all around the outside edges of the quilt. Finally, baste twice across the quilt—about a quarter from the top and a quarter from the bottom.

Remove the pins. Behold, your effort has produced a nice, neat package, and you have a sense of accomplishment that far outweights your aching back and, by now, purplish knees.

5. *Begin quilting at the center* of the quilt and work toward the outside edges (see "General quilting tips" on page 64).

Arrange the layers in the hoop so they are held taut. You may find the quilting stitch more difficult to do when the fabric is in a hoop, but don't be discouraged. You will quickly learn to make the stitches inside the hoop. Remember that regular, evenly spaced stitches are more important than very tiny ones. (You can even cheat a little and loosen the fabric within the hoop a bit to make it easier as you learn.)

Remember your thimble! Work with your left hand under the hoop and fabric. (Reverse this if you are left-handed.) Insert the needle with your right hand. Let the needle graze the tip of your left middle finger to be sure that all the thicknesses are caught, then push the needle back up with your left index finger. Try to take several stitches before you pull the needle through.

As work progresses and you near the edge of the quilt, it becomes somewhat difficult to keep your work taut because the fabric will not fill the entire hoop. This can be remedied by basting a piece of old sheeting to the edge of the quilt, then clamping the hoop to the extra fabric. If you'd rather not baste, you can use a smaller hoop (14" or 12") to help you quilt to the edges.

6. *Finish the edges.* This last step is described below.

FINISHING THE EDGES

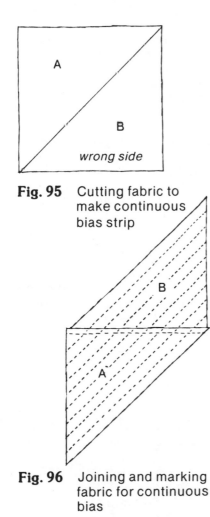

Fig. 95 Cutting fabric to make continuous bias strip

Fig. 96 Joining and marking fabric for continuous bias

The day will come when your quilting is done, and the edges must be finished. There are some choices here, too. We describe three.

1. *Use a separate binding.* This is a favorite way of finishing a quilt. Since the edges receive the most wear, they may have to be repaired later on. A separate binding can easily be replaced.

You need enough binding to go around the outside edge of the quilt. That's 396" (11 yds.) around a full-size quilt. Add about ¼ yd. (for a total of 11¼ yd.) so that there's plenty for easing around corners and for seam allowances.

A binding can be cut on the bias (our favorite way) or on the straight grain.

a. *If you decide to use bias binding,* it is helpful to make a continuous bias strip—one that's long enough to go around the whole quilt. You have enough extra sashing fabric to do this (that piece you labeled "Binding" back in Chapter 1).

To make a continuous strip

Fabric for bias strip	
twin	32" square
full	34" square
queen	35" square
king	36" square

of bias, use a square of fabric Check the chart above for the size you need.

Fold the square on a diagonal, and cut it from one corner to the other (Fig. 95). Fit the top edge against the bottom edge (Fig. 96). Stitch them, right sides together, with a ¼" seam. Press the seam to one side.

Beginning at the top bias edge, mark off 2½" widths (see broken lines on Fig. 96). These will be your cutting lines. You can draft a cardboard template, 2½" wide, to make the marking faster and easier.

Form a tube (Fig. 97), joining the straight edges, right sides together. Have each end of the tube extending a 2½" width beyond the other, and have pencil lines match-

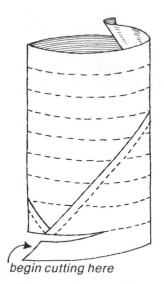

Fig. 97   Forming a bias tube

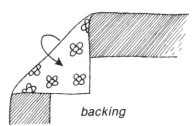

Fig. 98   Turning corner to begin miter

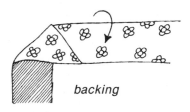

Fig. 99   Turning top edge for miter

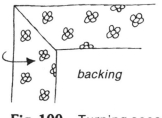

Fig. 100   Turning second edge to complete miter

ing where the seam will be stitched (¼" from the edges). Stitch a ¼" seam, and press it to one side.

Begin cutting at a 2½" extension along the pencil line, and continue cutting until you have one long strip of bias.

To attach the bias to the quilt, lay the bias on top of the quilt border, right sides together, with the outside edges even. Pin in place, easing bias around the corners. Stitch a ½" seam.

Fold the bias over the edge of the quilt and onto the backing. Turn under a ½" seam allowance, and hand-stitch the bias to the backing, covering the first line of stitching as you work.

b. *If you decide to use binding cut on the straight grain,* attach it just as you do bias binding, but end the strips at each corner. Fold the raw edges under to make neat finishes.

2. *Fold the border over the edge.* This simple finish is made by folding the border to the back of the quilt and sewing it in place. For this, trim the batting and the backing fabric along the outside edges to make them 1" narrower than the quilt top. Then fold the quilt border over the edge and onto the backing.

Note: If you quilt the border, you must plan ahead and keep your quilting stitches at least 1¼" away from the outside edges.

Miter each corner by making a diagonal fold across the corner and onto the back (Fig. 98). Turn down 1" on one side (Fig. 99). Then turn 1" on the adjoining side (Fig. 100) to form the miter.

Tuck under ½" seam allowances along the raw edges of the border. Hand-stitch the mitered edges together, and hand-stitch the border edges to the backing.

Note: You can reverse this procedure and fold the backing fabric over the edge to the front of the quilt.

3. *Hem at the edge.* This is another simple finish. Trim the border and backing so that they are even (the same size), then trim the batting to make it ½" narrower. Turn both border and backing fabrics ½" to the inside, and use a whipping stitch (Fig. 75) to sew them together.

Remove bastings—Admire!

Pull out the remaining basting stitches. Check the quilt top to make sure that all the quilting is finished, and that the edging is secure. Do your signature and date appear on the quilt?

Honestly appraise your work. Isn't it one of the most beautiful quilts that you have ever seen? You feel like calling the neighbors and asking them to come and see your masterpiece, don't you? Go ahead and call them. You have good reason to be proud of your work.

We know that your family and friends will think that you are fantastically clever to have learned quilting from a book. They probably are already deluging you with requests for pillows.

We hope you will go on to Part Two and begin plans for an Advanced Sampler Quilt—or maybe one of the variations we tell you about. We also hope that quilting has become a happy habit.

Extra quilting designs

Part Two

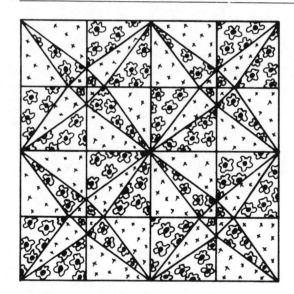

For advanced quilters

If your Beginner's Sampler Quilt is finished and your fingers are itching for a new project, we have some suggestions for you. Chapter 7 offers a variety of ideas for your next quilt, along with directions for making a handy tote bag using just one quilt block. We also tell you how to change the size of a block—helpful when you want to make something for a child's bed.

In Chapters 8 and 9, you'll find a dozen different quilt block designs, each requiring more skill and time than any of the beginner's blocks. Even an experienced quilter will spend three or four hours on a single block. These 12 designs can be made into an attractive Advanced Sampler Quilt.

We hope you won't attempt the advanced quilt blocks until you have mastered all the designs in Part One. (No matter how tempting diamonds may look, they aren't easy.) Once your skill is perfected, however, go ahead. When you can turn out these advanced blocks, you have truly arrived in the world of quilting.

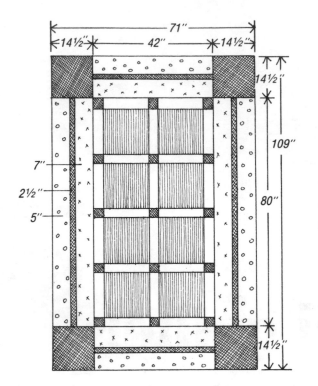

Fig. 101 Layout for Advanced
Sampler Quilt, twin size

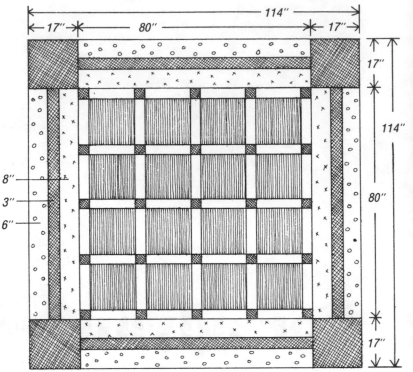

Fig. 102 Layout for Advanced
Sampler Quilt, king size

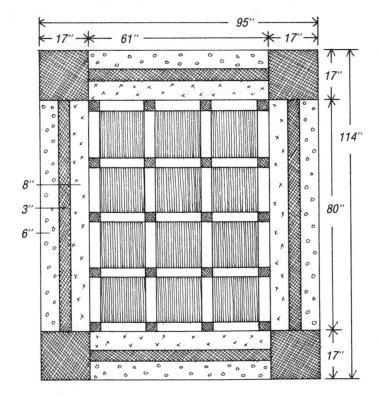

Fig. 103 Layout for Advanced
Sampler Quilt, queen size

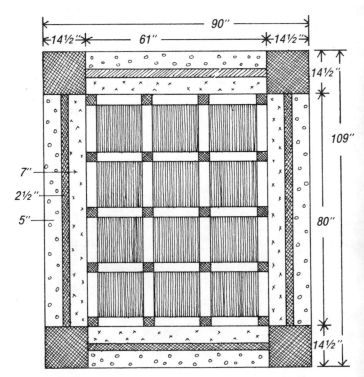

Fig. 104 Layout for Advanced
Sampler Quilt, full size

7 Choose your next project

There are many ways to make a quilt, and this chapter lists a few possibilities. We start with our Advanced Sampler Quilt, shown on plate 16. This quilt displays all the patchwork block designs.

We also have suggestions for making quilts that repeat a single design. With some of these, you might want to change the block size, and we'll tell you how to do that.

If you're interested in a quick project, we offer directions for making a tote bag. This lets you show off one perfect block.

Why not read through the chapter before you decide what to quilt next?

AN ADVANCED SAMPLER QUILT

The patchwork blocks in the next two chapters are more intricate than those you made for the Beginner's Sampler Quilt, but don't be dismayed. The earlier blocks introduced techniques that will help you master the new ones.

You'll note that fewer blocks are set for the Advanced Quilt than for the Beginner's Quilt. (See layouts in Figs. 101-104.) For example, only 12 blocks are set in a full-size quilt. This places most of the blocks on top of the bed where they will be prominently displayed.

The Advanced Sampler Quilt also has fancier sashing and border sections. The sashing is 4" wide and combines two different prints to create small corner squares. The border uses three prints and has four large corner squares.

Fabric needed

For fabrics in our Advanced Quilt, we concentrated on three basic prints, using them in the sashing, the border and in some blocks. With these, we used a few other prints and three solid colors.

The chart on the next page lists the yardage needed for each size quilt and includes enough fabric to complete all 12 advanced blocks. *Note:* Some border sections may have to be pieced.

Backing and batting yardages are the same as for the Beginner's Sampler Quilt; refer to Chapter 6.

Making the sashing

You will need to draft two templates—a 4x4" square A and a 4x15" rectangle B. Check the quilt layout for your size quilt to find the number of sashing pieces you need.

On the *wrong* side of the fabric, trace and cut the pieces, adding ½" seam allowances.

Follow Fig. 105 for assembling sashing pieces and quilt blocks for Rows 1-3.

Follow Fig. 106 for assembling sashing pieces and quilt blocks for Row 4 (bottom row of quilt).

Yardage for advanced blocks and quilt top				
Type of fabric, 45″ wide	twin	full (double)	queen	king
Print for sashing, bias binding and some blocks	2 yd.	3½ yd.	3½ yd.	4½ yd.
Print for corner squares of sashing	½ yd.	¾ yd.	¾ yd.	1 yd.
Assorted prints and solids for blocks, ¼ to ½ yd. each	2 yd.	3 yd.	3 yd.	4 yd.
Three prints for border:				
Inside strip	1½ yd.	1½ yd.	1½ yd	2 yd.
Middle strip	2 yd.	2¼ yd.	2½ yd.	3 yd.
Outside strip	2½ yd.	2½ yd.	2½ yd.	3½ yd.
Number of blocks needed	8	12	12	16

Making the border

Refer to your quilt layout. You'll find dimensions for each border section (be sure to add ½″ seam allowances when cutting fabric).

Sew the three border fabrics together to form each section. Add a corner square to each end of the top and bottom sections.

After the rows and border sections are assembled, refer to Chapter 6 for finishing the quilt. (Use the single-row or hoop method for quilting.)

Note: Before you cut any backing pieces, check the measurements of your quilt row or quilt top. There may be an inch or so difference in some measurements between the Beginner's Quilt and the Advanced Quilt for the same-size bed.

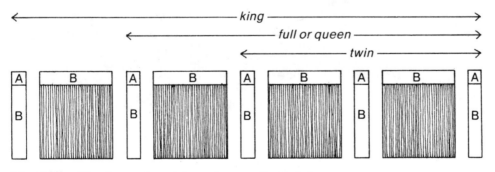

Fig. 105 Blocks and sashing pieces, Rows 1-3

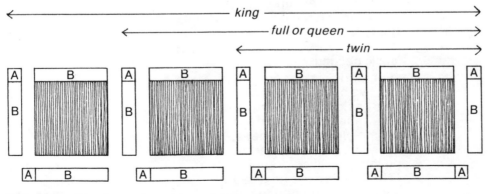

Fig. 106 Blocks and sashing pieces, Row 4

QUILTS WITH A SINGLE DESIGN

Most quilts are made with only one patchwork design. repeated over and over. Perhaps you found a favorite block in Part One. Or you may discover a design you like in the next two chapters. If so, concentrate on that design and complete enough blocks for a big quilt—or a small one. Then set the blocks with sashing, without sashing or in a checkerboard fashion.

Using sashing

To set the blocks with sashing, follow the layout and directions for either the Beginner's Sampler Quilt or the Advanced Sampler Quilt. An example of a single-design quilt (Grandmother's Flower Garden) set with sashing is shown on plate 5.

Omitting sashing

To set blocks without sashing, simply stitch the blocks together. When two blocks meet, often lines connect and begin to form new patterns. You will be amazed at the unexpected designs that emerge. A particularly interesting example is shown on plate 9 using Jacob's Ladder.

One of the advanced designs found in Chapter 8, Crossed Canoes, forms a smashing and very contemporary kaleidoscopic design when repeated without sashing. You can see the effect on plate 14, where we have repeated the basic design four times.

A checkerboard effect

To set blocks in checkerboard fashion, alternate patchwork with same-size squares of fabric in a print or solid color. If you use a solid color, you can duplicate the patchwork design on these squares in quilting stitches.

QUILTS FOR CHILDREN

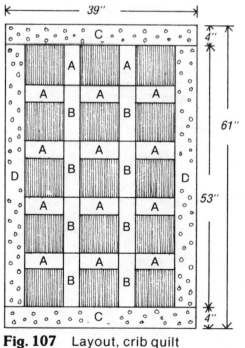

Fig. 107 Layout, crib quilt

Blocks, 9" square

A—sashing pieces, 2x9"   C—border pieces, 4x39"
B—sashing pieces, 2x11"   D—border pieces, 4x53"

Note: Add ½" seam allowances when cutting fabric

To make a small quilt for a baby's crib or a child's bed, you may want to use smaller size blocks. (Directions for changing a block size begin on page 80.)

Many patterns in this book will look at home in a child's room, especially if you choose cheerful colors. You'll find examples of children's quilts on plate 8. On the Heart quilt, one heart is edged with lace and personalized with embroidery.

With a little figuring, you can determine the size and number of blocks, and the size of sashing pieces and borders you need to put together any size quilt. As a suggestion for a crib quilt, we offer the layout in Fig. 107. This uses 15 blocks (9"-square) with 2" sashing and a 4" border. Overall dimensions are 39x61". (A standard crib-size mattress is 27x52", and a crib quilt usually runs 40x60".)

HANDY TOTE BAG

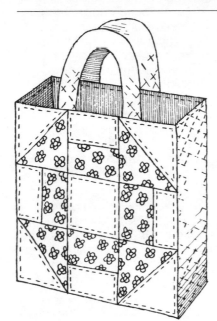

Fig. 108   Tote bag

Fig. 109   Stitching handle

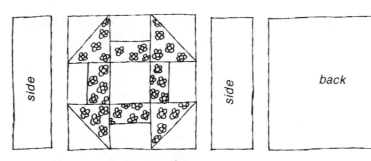

Fig. 110   Arranging sections

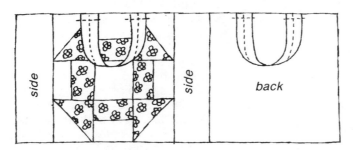

Fig. 111   Positioning handles

You already know how to turn one patchwork block into a pillow top (Chapter 4). A quilted tote bag (Fig. 108) is another way to use extra quilt blocks for yourself and for gifts. Examples are shown in color on plate 13.

To make a tote, you will need:

• *1 quilted patchwork block* for the front of the bag. Stack and baste layers—block (right side up) on top, batting in the middle, muslin on the bottom—then quilt. (Refer to "General quilting tips," Chapter 6.)

• *½ yd. quilted fabric, 45"* wide, (purchased) for the outside pieces and handles.

• *½ yd. regular (unquilted) fabric, 45"* wide, for the lining.

Note: Some stores carry the same prints and solid colors in both quilted and regular yardage.

Cutting the fabric

Use two templates—a 15" square and a 4x15" rectangle. On the *wrong* side of the quilted fabric, trace and cut (adding ½" seam allowances):

    15" square — 1
       piece (for the back)
    4x15" rectangle — 5
       pieces (for handles, side
       panels and bottom)

On the *wrong* side of the lining fabric, place the 4x15" rectangle ½" from the selvage edge (this is the seam allowance). Trace and cut one piece, which will be used to line the bottom of the bag. (Be sure to allow ½" seam allowances on all sides.)

On the remaining lining fabric, mark and cut one large section, 16x39" (this includes seam allowances).

Assembling the bag

1. Use two rectangles of quilted fabric to make the handles. Fold each strip in half lengthwise, right sides together, and stitch a ½" seam (Fig. 109). Turn to the right side. Center the seam line on one side and press.

2. Arrange quilted pieces, right side up, following Fig. 110. Stitch together to make one flat piece.

3. Place the handles in position on the right side of the square sections, measuring in 3" from the seam lines (Fig. 111). Keep handle seams up, and raw edges even with the top edge of the bag. Stitch across edges of handles to secure.

4. Place the 16x39" lining fabric on top of the quilted fabric, right sides together. Stitch the top seam, using a ½" seam allowance, and going over the handles. Press the seam open.

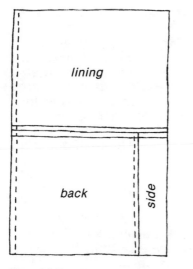

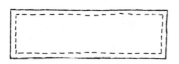

Fig. 112   Closing side seam

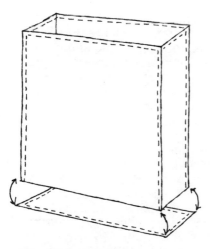

Fig. 113   Bottom of bag

Fig. 114   Attaching bottom to tote

5. Place tote and lining flat on a table, right side up. Fold the fabric in half, vertically, right sides together. Pin the raw edges along the side, and stitch (Fig. 112).

6. To assemble the bottom of the bag, place the lining rectangle on top of the quilted rectangle, wrong sides together. Stitch ½" from the edge. (Fig. 113.)

7. Pin the bottom section to the quilted fabric of the bag, with right (quilted) sides together (Fig. 114). Keep lining fabric of bag out of the way.

Match the corners of the bottom rectangle to the seams of the bag. Sew together, one side at a time. Try to keep the corners square.

8. Fold the bag lining into place. Turn under the seam allowance, and hand-sew to the bottom section. Turn the bag right side out.

9. Add a line of hand quilting around the top of the bag to hold the lining in place.

HOW TO CHANGE BLOCK SIZE

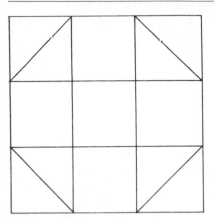
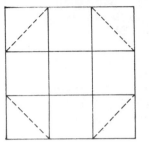

Fig. 115 Copying a nine-patch block

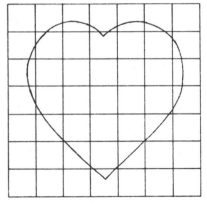
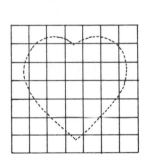

Fig. 116 Copying a free-form design

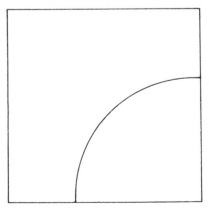

Fig. 117 Drawing a new curve

For some projects, such as a child's quilt, you may want to change the size of a block. All blocks in this book are 15" square when finished. Some blocks, however, include a special sashing or border so that the center design is actually smaller (Sunbonnet Sue is an example).

Here are ways to change a block size:

For a pieced-work block based on square units, draw a new block the size you wish (perhaps 9" square) on a large sheet of paper. Then divide this block into the same number of units contained in the original block. (For example, divide a nine-patch block into nine small squares, and a four-patch block into 16 small squares.)

Draw the design in the new block (see Fig. 115). This gives you patterns for making new templates.

Free-form shapes such as the heart can be transferred using a grid system (Fig. 116). Trace the original design on a square, then divide this into 1" squares. (You can use graph paper with ¼" divisions, then mark off the 1" units.)

Draw a new square the size you want, and divide this into the same number of segments you have in the original design.

Transfer the pattern, square by square, from the original to the corresponding square on the new block. Unless pieces must fit together precisely, a little variation in shape and size will not matter.

For curved designs, such as Dresden Plate, shorten or lengthen the petal design to fit your new block. For Drunkard's Path (Fig. 143, p. 97), use a compass to draw a curve on the new square unit, intersecting the bottom and side about two-thirds across (Fig. 117).

8 Test your skill on advanced piecing

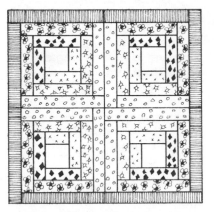

Fig. 118 Log Cabin
(See also plate 11)

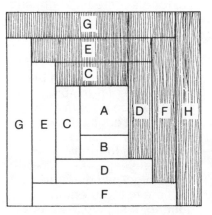

Fig. 119 Guide for piecing block

The quilt blocks in this chapter require the same basic techniques as the beginner's blocks— trace, cut, pin-baste, stitch, trim and finger-press. However, as you work your way through the chapter, you also will find new techniques to challenge you.

INTRICATE PIECING

Each of the two quilt blocks that follow requires a special order of construction. The pieces don't just fall neatly into rows of squares.

LOG CABIN

Let's start with a very old design shown in Fig. 118. Colonists used red fabric in the center square to signify the fire on the hearth. They surrounded this with strips or "logs" of light and dark fabrics arranged to form an overall design. In our block, the basic design (Fig. 119) is repeated four times, with the light fabrics grouped at the center.

Patterns for Log Cabin are on page 89. You will need to make eight templates—one square and seven rectangles. Be sure to label them.

Select seven fabrics—one solid color and six prints, three light and three dark.

On the *wrong* side of the fabric, trace and cut (adding ½″ seam allowances):

    A—4 of solid color
    B—4 of light print No. 1
    C—4 of light print No. 1
    C—4 of dark print No. 1
    D—4 of dark print No. 1
    D—4 of light print No. 2
    E—4 of light print No. 2
    E—4 of dark print No. 2
    F—4 of dark print No. 2
    F—4 of light print No. 3
    G—4 of light print No. 3
    G—4 of dark print No. 3
    H—4 of dark print No. 3

Arrange all the pieces in front of you, according to Fig. 118, with light and dark prints in position. Then work with one unit (one-fourth of the

Fig. 120   Ocean Waves
with quilted center
(See also plate 11)

Fig. 121   Forming outside
row

Fig. 122   Forming inside row

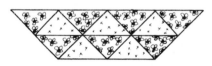

Fig. 123   Joining the two
rows

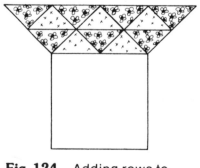

Fig. 124   Adding rows to
center square

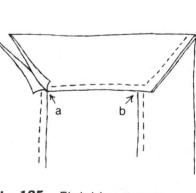

Fig. 125   Finishing corner
seams

block) at a time, adding the logs clockwise and following the letters in order (Fig. 119). Pick up A and add B. Then add C (light print), and continue working around the square. (You first encountered this technique when you made Jean's Rose, remember?)

Repeat the process to make three more squares. Remember to trim finished seams to just under ¼". Arrange the squares according to Fig. 118, and join them to form the final block.

OCEAN WAVES

This block has a solid color square surrounded by two rows of triangles, alternating in light and dark prints (Fig. 120). The square is a perfect showplace for a quilting design, and we have chosen an historic one called the Double Feathered Plate. It's similar to the one used on the quilted pillow in Chapter 4.

For Ocean Waves, you'll need two templates—square A and small triangle B. Pat-terns are on page 90. Be sure to copy the Double Feathered Plate quilting design onto the square A template, and go over the design with a felt-tip pen.

Select three fabrics—one light solid color and two prints, a light and a dark.

On the *wrong* side of the fabric, trace and cut (adding ½" seam allowances):

    A—1 of light solid color
    B—24 of light print
    B—24 of dark print

Arrange the pieces in front of you, following Fig. 120. Begin with the top outside row and join the triangles (Fig. 121). Then join the triangles on the inside row (Fig. 122). Sew the two rows together (Fig. 123).

Next, work with the triangles on the left side of the block (see Fig. 120). Note that the light and dark triangles are reversed in posi-tion.

Repeat to form rows of triangles on the remaining two sides, then sew the rows together. Keep an eye on Fig. 120 for placement of light and dark triangles.

Sew each triangle section to the center square (Fig. 124), stitching only to the end of the pencil lines marked on the wrong side of the fabric. There will be a seam allow-ance left at each corner (Fig. 125-a). Join these seam allowances to form corner diagonal seams (Fig. 125-b).

The block is completed, and it's time to transfer the quilting design to the center square. Place the template with the Double Feathered Plate design under the fabric. Anchor the layers, and trace the design with a No. 5H or 6H pencil. The design will be worked later when the blocks are assembled and you are ready to do the quilting.

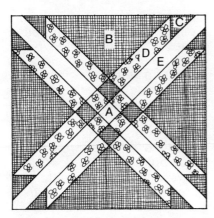

Fig. 126   Mexican Star
(See also plate 11)

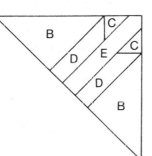

Fig. 127   Corner of block

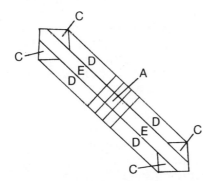

Fig. 128   Center diagonal of block

REVERSE PIECING

For some pieced work, you place a template on the fabric and trace around one side, then flip the template over and trace around the reverse side. This is easy to do, but it is also easy to mix up the fabric pieces. Here are a few quilt blocks that let you practice reverse piecing.

MEXICAN STAR

The beautiful design in Fig. 126 is sometimes called Mexican Cross and was probably inspired by the Mexican War that took place between 1846 and 1848. Examples of quilts made in this design during the war years are found in all sections of the country.

Before you do anything, look at Fig. 127. This is a corner section of the block (upper right), and the D pieces illustrate reverse piecing. The first D, at left, is traced around one side of the template, and the second D is traced around the reverse side of the same template. All other pieces are traced in the standard way.

First make the five templates from patterns on page 91, and label them. Then select three fabrics— two solid colors and one print.

On the *wrong* side of the fabric, trace and cut (adding ½″ seam allowances):

    A—1 of solid color No. 1
    A—4 of solid color No. 2
    A—4 of print
    B—4 of solid color No. 2
    C—8 of solid color No. 2
    D—4 of print
    D (reversed)—4 of print
    E—4 of solid color No. 1

Lay the pieces for one section of the block in front of you, following Fig. 127. To assemble, first sew the C pieces to the D pieces. Then sew a B to a C/D. Add E, then another C/D, then another B to complete the triangle. Repeat the process to form a second triangle.

Now work with pieces in the center diagonal section, arranged accordingly to Fig. 128. Sew pieces together to form rows, then join the rows.

Finally, join the two corner triangles to the center section to complete the block.

Fig. 129   54-40 or Fight
with quilted sashing
(See also plate 11)

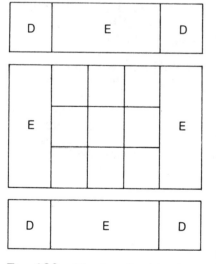

Fig. 130   Piecing the block

54-40 OR FIGHT

The famous old quilt block in Fig. 129 signifies the interest that early quilters took in political events of the country. The name was a political slogan used by Democrats in the presidential election of 1844, and referred to proposed boundries of the United States.

You may recognize the center design as a nine-patch. However, its small checkerboard squares and reverse templates make it a challenge worthy of an advanced quilter. We framed the basic design with sashing that you can quilt later in a scroll design.

Make the templates from patterns on page 92, copying the scroll design onto template E so you can transfer it to the fabric.

Select four fabrics—three solid colors and one print. On the *wrong* side of the fabric, trace and cut (adding ½" seam allowances):

    A—10 of solid color No. 1
    A—10 of solid color No. 2
    B—4 of solid color No. 1
    C—4 of print
    C (reversed)—4 of print
    D—4 of solid color No. 2
    E—4 of solid color No. 3

Arrange the pieces in front of you and begin assembling the five checkerboard squares.

To save time if you are using a machine, first handle all the square A pieces in pairs. Pin two adjoining A squares right sides together. Feed them, a pair at a time, under the presser foot, leaving a length of thread between each pair. Then cut the threads to separate the units, trim the seam allowances and finger press. Position the pairs according to Fig. 129.

Complete the five checkerboard squares. Be sure you pin-baste the pieces together carefully to keep your work accurate, and finger-press the stitched seams.

Next, sew a star point C to a triangle B. Add the remaining star point C-reversed to complete a square. Repeat this process to make three more star-point squares.

When all the nine-patch squares are completed, arrange them in front of you according to Fig. 129. Notice that there is a definite pattern for the checkerboard squares. Each color marches diagonally in the same direction.

Sew the squares together to form three rows. Then sew the rows together to complete the nine-patch square. Pay particular attention to the star points. Be sure they line up with the seams on the center checkerboard square. A little extra care will repay you with a handsome quilt block.

The sashing comes next. Sew a square D to each end of a rectangle E for the top row (Fig. 130). Repeat to make the bottom row.

Sew a rectangle E to both the right and left sides of the nine-patch square. Then add the top and bottom rows of sashing to complete the block.

Center the scroll design on each E sashing piece and transfer the design for quilting later. (See "Extra quilting lines" on page 61.)

Wasn't that an interesting challenge? There is such a sense of accomplishment when you successfully complete these advanced blocks.

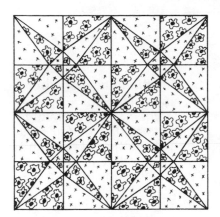

Fig. 131 Crossed Canoes
(See also plate 14)

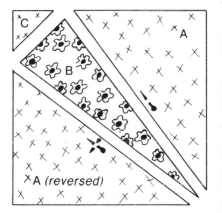

Fig. 132 Using pins to mark triangles

Have patience

If you ever reach a point with one of the advanced designs where you just can't get the block together correctly, go back to the first step and lay the pieces out on a table to form the design. Then take a break.

Go for a walk, play a hand of solitaire, or do something else you thoroughly enjoy. While you are away from the quilt pieces, your mind will be busy trying to solve the puzzle. When you go back to the block, you will be able to put it together.

CROSSED CANOES

When this traditional quilt block was first developed, waterways were the lifeblood of American travel and commerce. The early quilters probably modeled the design in Fig. 131 after Indian vessels.

Crossed Canoes is an optical illusion. The pattern is developed with straight lines, but the overall effect is that of curved lines. Our version repeats the basic design four times, and you can begin to see the kaleidoscopic effect it creates. This block offers you more practice in handling small pieces and in reversing templates.

Take a close look at the basic design (one-fourth of the block). There are an equal number of light and dark pieces, and those pieces are arranged to replace each other in adjoining squares. The squares are said to be "robbed" or "replaced."

Make the templates—three triangles—from patterns on page 93. Then select two print fabrics, one light and one dark.

On the *wrong* side of the fabric, trace and cut (adding ½" seam allowances):
A—8 of light print
A—8 of dark print
A (reversed)—8 of light print
A (reversed)—8 of dark print
B—8 of light print
B—8 of dark print
C—8 of light print
C—8 of dark print

Note: When you cut the A pieces, place one pin along the seam line that will join the B triangle (Fig. 132). When you cut the A-reversed pieces, place two pins, crossed, along the seam line that will join the B triangle. You wouldn't believe how easy it is to confuse the A pieces, and the pins really help keep them in order.

Arrange the pieces in front of you according to Fig. 131, and work with four small squares that form one-fourth of the big block.

To assemble one small square (Fig. 132), sew a light triangle C to a dark triangle B. Then add a light A and a light A-reversed. This completes a square.

Make three more small squares. Watch the color placement carefully, reversing the light and dark pieces following Fig. 131. Join the four small squares to make one larger square (one-fourth of the block). Pin the pieces together carefully so that the points of the pattern meet. Good pinning is as important as the sewing.

Join the remaining pieces to form small squares, then complete three more large squares. Finally, join the four large squares to complete the block.

Congratulations! You have just created your own optical illusion.

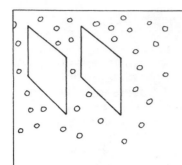

Fig. 133 Cutting diamonds, method 1

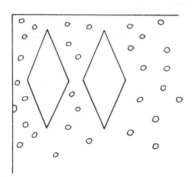

Fig. 134 Cutting diamonds, method 2

DIAMONDS

We finally come to a section you have been waiting for—diamonds. Our first block has a star made of eight large diamonds. The second block also has a star, but it uses nine times as many diamonds as the first block. You will really know about diamonds when you've finished these two blocks.

Two ways to cut diamonds

There are two methods for cutting diamonds from fabric, and you may use either one. After you choose, however, be consistent for each project.

Method 1. Place two straight sides of the template on the straight grain (Fig. 133). Each diamond has two edges on the straight grain and two edges on the bias.

Method 2. Place the template on the fabric, with the widest part of the diamond on the straight grain (Fig. 134). All four edges are bias. However, they are not true bias (45°), and they will not stretch as much as true bias.

Sewing diamonds together

If you cut the fabric following Method 1, sew a straight edge of one diamond to a bias edge of another. (If you can't see the straight grain, determine it by gently tugging the edge. The bias edge will stretch, while the straight grain will remain firm.) To machine-stitch, have the bias edge on the bottom layer.

If you cut diamonds following Method 2, all edges are the same. Handle them carefully to avoid stretching.

For all diamonds, *sew only on the traced pencil lines.* Do not stitch into the seam allowances, or your diamonds won't have nice points.

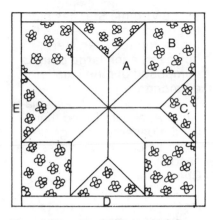

Fig. 135 Eight-Pointed Star
(See also plate 14)

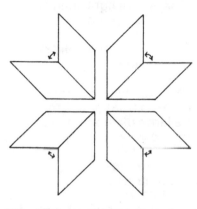

Fig. 136 Joining pairs of diamonds

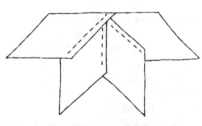

Fig. 137 Pressing all seams in same direction

EIGHT-POINTED STAR

Our pattern in Fig. 135 uses a solid color for the star and the narrow sashing, with a print for the remaining pieces.

Make five templates for the block. Copy diamond A, square B and triangle C from the patterns on page 110. Then draft two rectangles for the borders—1-$^1/_8$x12 ¾" (D) and 1-$^1/_8$x15" (E).

On the *wrong* side of the fabric, trace and cut (adding ½" seam allowances):

  A—8 of solid color
  B—4 of print
  C—4 of print
  D—2 of solid color
  E—2 of solid color

Work with the pieces in this order:

1. Arrange the diamond pieces in front of you, following the diagram (Fig. 135) for the block.

2. Pick up two diamonds and pin them together (Fig. 136). Sew along the traced pencil lines only (not to the raw edges). Then trim the seam allowance to 1/8" and finger-press. Pin and sew the remaining three pairs of diamonds, trim the seams and finger-press.

3. Join two pairs of diamonds to complete the top half of the star. Repeat to complete the bottom half. Finger-press or iron the seams so they all go in the same direction (Fig. 137).

4. Pin the two star halves together. This sewing must be precise, and we recommend that you do it by hand. Sew from one end to the middle, beginning on the pencil lines, not the outside raw edge. When you come to the middle, do not catch the intersecting seam allowances. Lift them out of the way and sew under them—along the pencil lines. This prevents a lump from forming right in the middle of your beautiful star. Continue sewing to the opposite end of the pencil lines.

5. After the star is sewed together, arrange the squares B and the triangles C around it (Fig. 135). Work with one side of each star point, attaching it to the adjoining square or triangle (Fig. 138); sew only on the pencil lines.

Then connect the remaining side of each star point to the adjoining piece. Be careful. This is where three seams come together.

6. Add sashing pieces D to the top and bottom of the star block. Then add sashing pieces E to the sides.

There! You have a framed Eight-Pointed Star. You can see why we left diamonds for the advanced section. Aren't you pleased with the professional quality of your work?

Fig. 138 Adding squares and triangles

Fig. 139 **Virginia Star**
(See also plate 14)

VIRGINIA STAR

This is a star of great beauty—and 72 separate diamonds. The quilt pattern in Fig. 139 is also referred to as Harvest Sun, and it has two spectacular relatives called Lone Star and Star of Bethlehem.

The Virginia Star has eight large star points just like the Eight-Pointed Star. Here, however, each large point is composed of nine smaller diamonds.

Make three templates—diamond A, square B and triangle C from patterns on page 95. A plastic coffee-can cover is handy for the diamond. Choose three fabrics in solid colors (light, medium, dark) for the star, and one print for the background.

On the *wrong* side of the fabric, trace and cut (adding ½″ seam allowances):

    A—16 of light solid color
    A—32 of medium solid
      color
    A—24 of dark solid color
    B—4 of print
    C—4 of print

Arrange nine diamond pieces in front of you to form one large diamond, following Fig. 140.

We're back to piecing rows. Pin-baste two diamonds together on the pencil lines (Fig. 141), then stitch from raw edge to raw edge. Complete three diagonal rows (Fig. 142).

Now sew the rows together to complete one large diamond. Watch those seams as they come together.

Repeat this process to piece seven more large diamonds.

To complete the block, follow Steps 1-5 under Eight-Pointed Star.

You've come a long way since the nine-patch, haven't you? Maybe you have even joined some of us who aspire to make a complete quilt of the Virginia Star design someday.

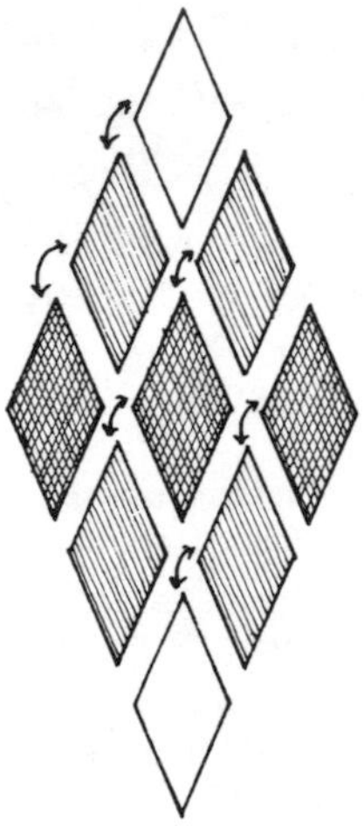

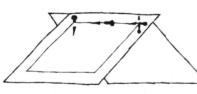

Fig. 140 Arranging small diamonds in rows

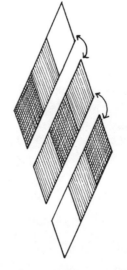

Fig. 141 Pin-basting diamonds

Fig. 142 Joining rows of diamonds

Patterns

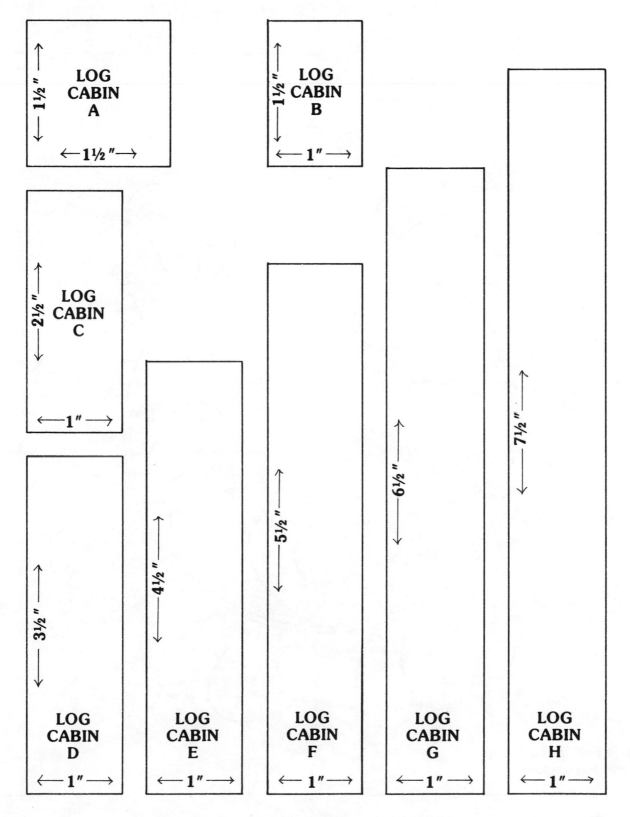

LOG CABIN A — 1½" × 1½"

LOG CABIN B — 1½" × 1"

LOG CABIN C — 2½" × 1"

LOG CABIN D — 3½" × 1"

LOG CABIN E — 4½" × 1"

LOG CABIN F — 5½" × 1"

LOG CABIN G — 6½" × 1"

LOG CABIN H — 7½" × 1"

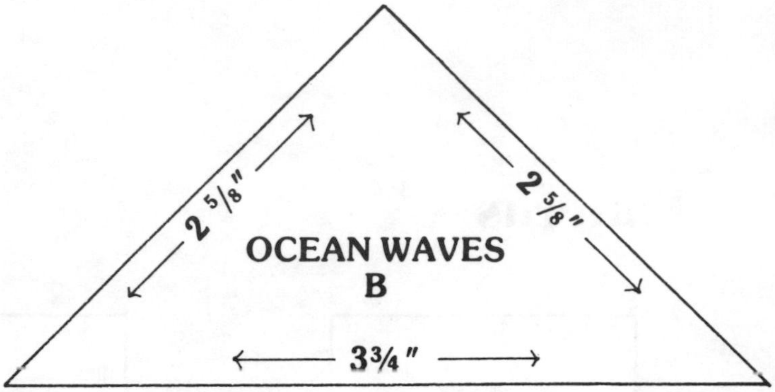

**OCEAN WAVES
B**

2 ⁵/₈ " 2 ⁵/₈ "

3¾ "

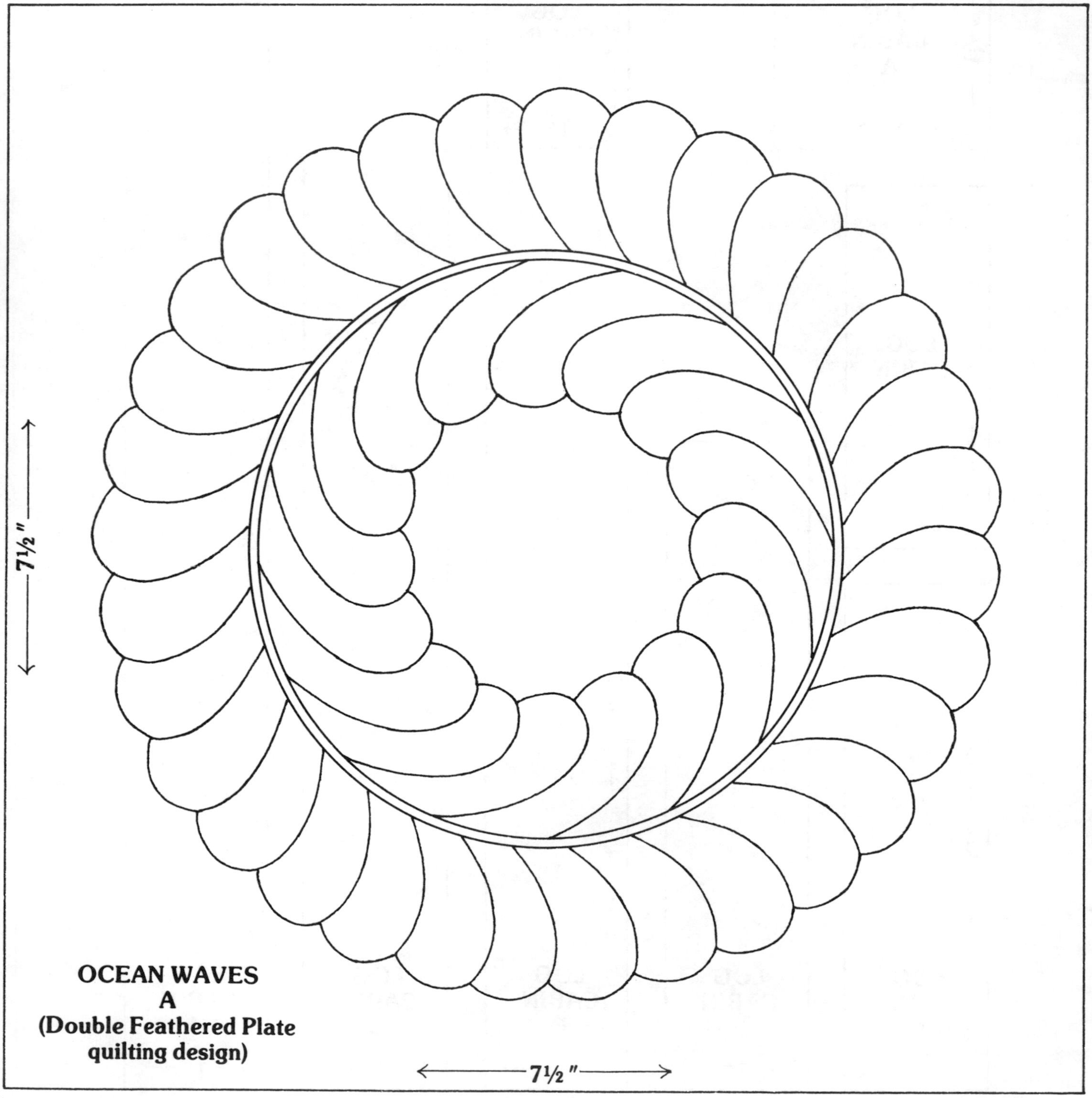

7½ "

**OCEAN WAVES
A
(Double Feathered Plate
quilting design)**

7½ "

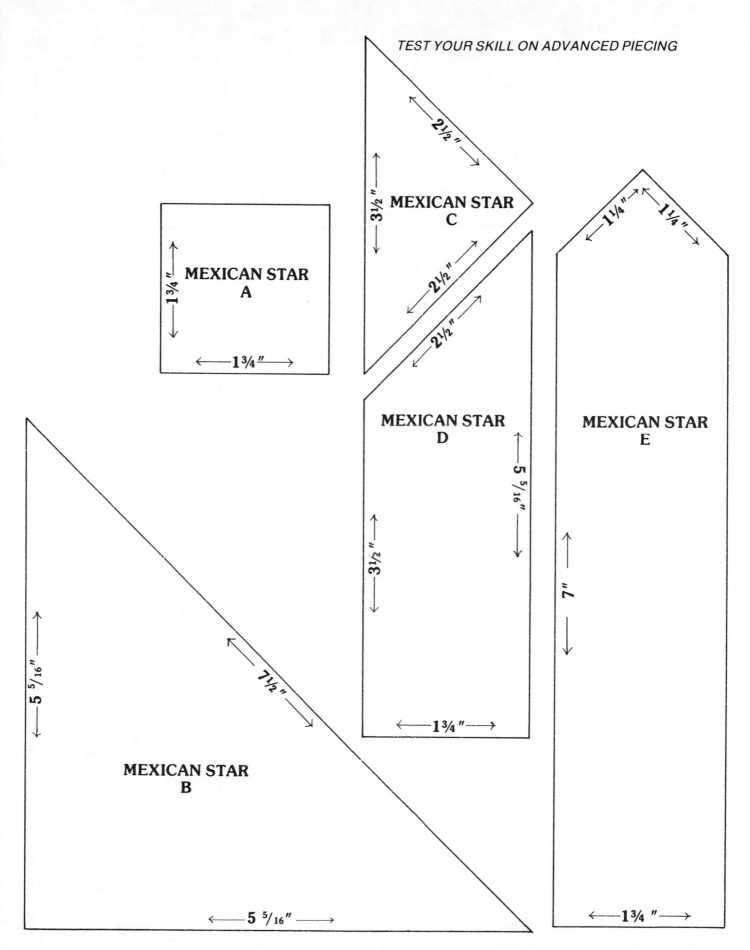

MEXICAN STAR
A

1¾"
1¾"

MEXICAN STAR
C

2½"
3½"
2½"
2½"

MEXICAN STAR
D

3½"
5 5/16"
1¾"

MEXICAN STAR
E

1¼"
1¼"
7"
1¾"

MEXICAN STAR
B

5 5/16"
7½"
5 5/16"

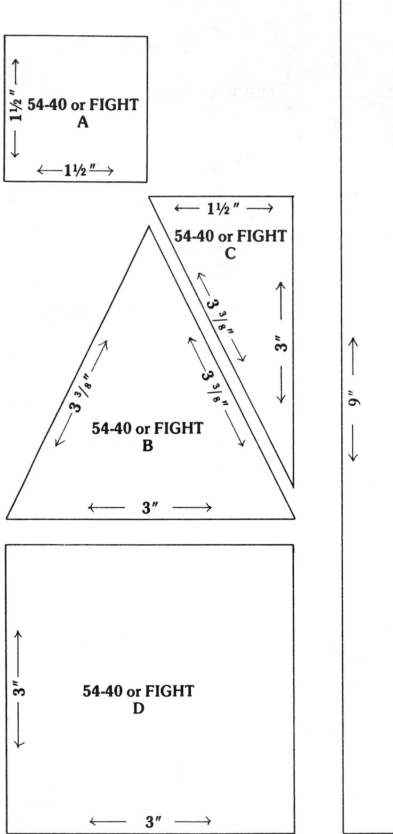

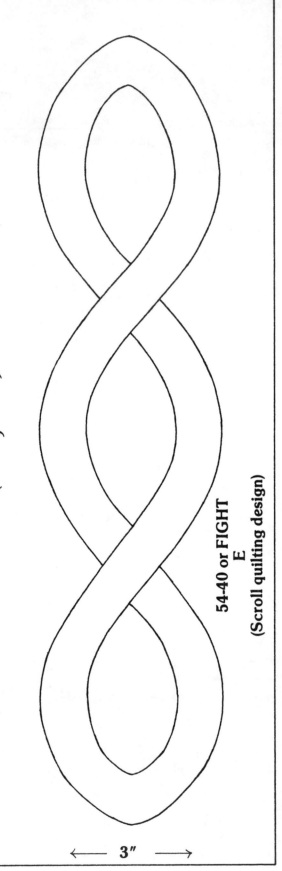

54-40 or FIGHT
A

54-40 or FIGHT
C

54-40 or FIGHT
B

54-40 or FIGHT
D

54-40 or FIGHT
E
(Scroll quilting design)

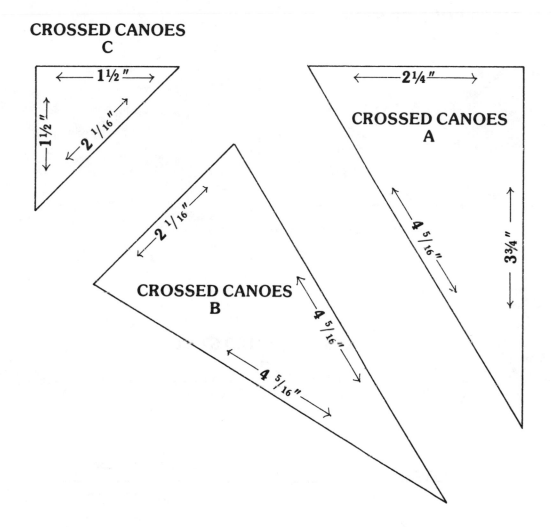

CROSSED CANOES
C

← 1½ " →

1½ "

2 ¹/₁₆"

CROSSED CANOES
A

← 2¼" →

4 ⁵/₁₆"

3¾ "

CROSSED CANOES
B

2 ¹/₁₆"

4 ⁵/₁₆"

4 ⁵/₁₆ "

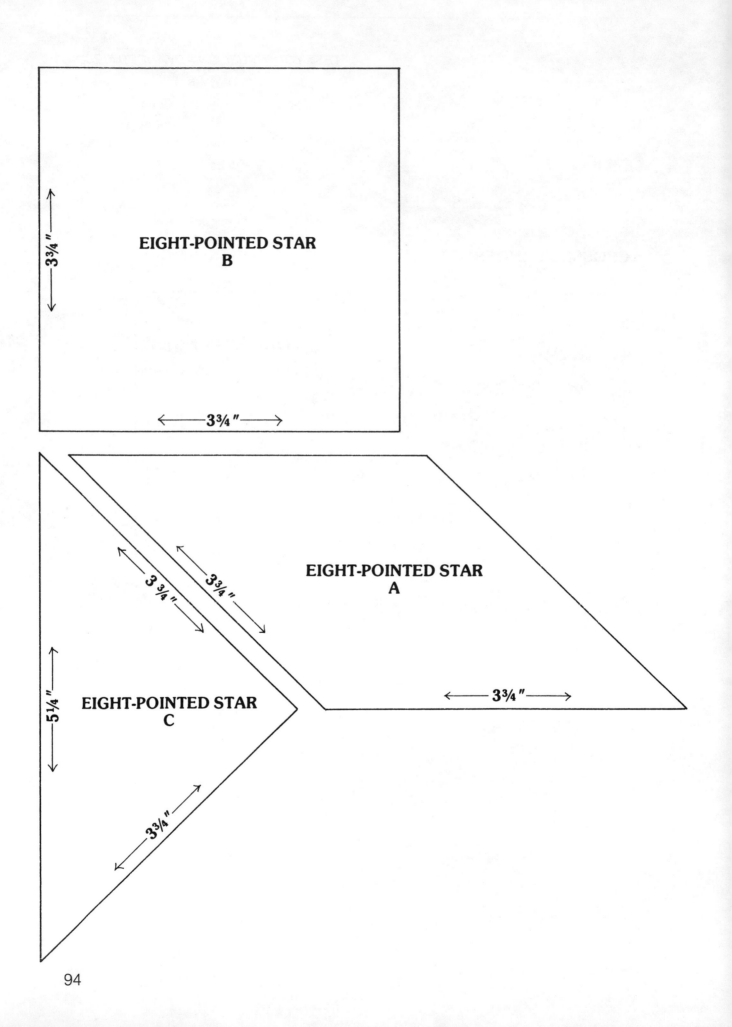

EIGHT-POINTED STAR
B

3¾ "

3¾ "

EIGHT-POINTED STAR
A

3¾ "

3¾ "

3¾ "

EIGHT-POINTED STAR
C

5¼ "

3¾ "

3¾ "

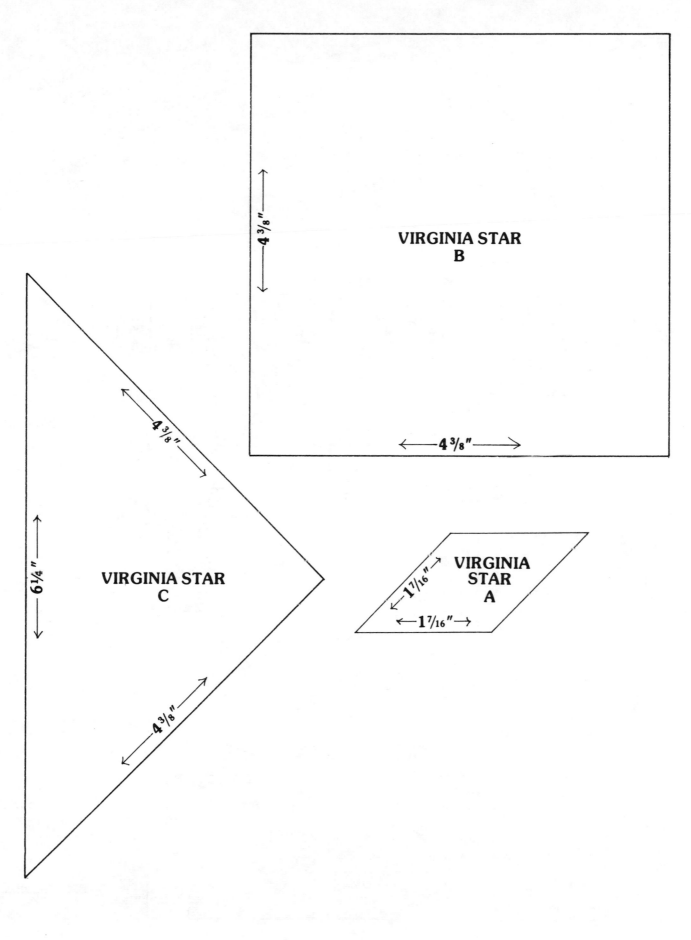

VIRGINIA STAR
B

4 3/8 "

4 3/8"

VIRGINIA STAR
C

6 1/4 "

4 3/8 "

4 3/8"

VIRGINIA
STAR
A

1 7/16 "

1 7/16"

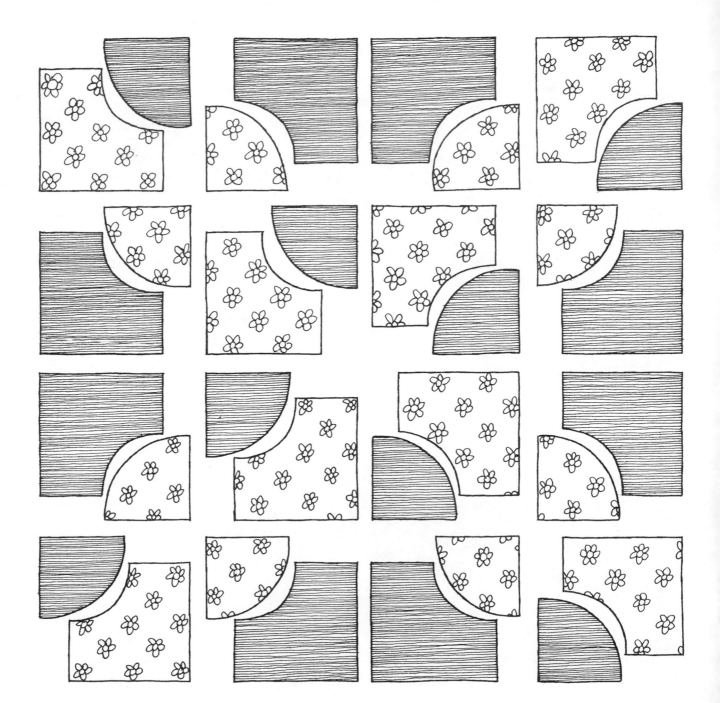

9 Conquer curves and paper work

We've saved patterns using curves and diamonds for the last five blocks. It takes skillful handling to keep curved edges smooth and even, and you'll learn how in both pieced work and paper work.

One block combines curves and diamonds—a real challenge. Another block introduces a new diamond shape.

CURVED PIECING

Not all pieced work is done with straight lines. Some patterns have curved pieces, and these don't go together as easily as straight edges. Curves are going to be a new learning experience for you. You should use a compass for accuracy, even when you trace patterns from the book.

DRUNKARD'S PATH

In colonial times the design shown in Fig. 143 was seldom made for a boy's bed. There was a superstition that a quilt made of the Drunkard's Path might cause the boy to develop an unhealthy interest in strong drink. The design also is known as Fool's Puz-

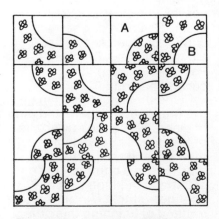

Fig. 143   Drunkard's Path
(See also plate 14)

zle, Country Husband, Country Roads and Pumpkin Vine.

You will need to make two templates, and both have curves. Patterns are on page 103.

Choose two fabrics—a solid color and a print. Place templates on the *wrong* side of the fabric, with the straight sides of the templates on the straight grain. Trace and cut (adding ½″ seam allowances):
  A—8 of solid color
  A—8 of print
  B—8 of solid color
  B—8 of print

Joining the curves

First stay-stitch the concave (inside) curve on each A piece, as in Fig. 144. Use machine stitches or tiny hand stitches just outside the pen-

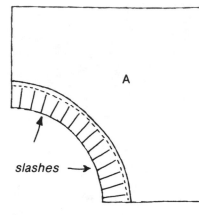

Fig. 144 Concave curve

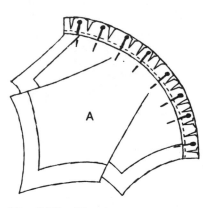

Fig. 145 Pinning curves together

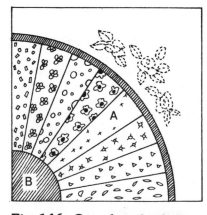

Fig. 146 Grandmother's Fan
(See also plate 15)

cil line in the seam allowance. This will keep the fabric from fraying as you stretch it to fit the matching convex (outward) curve of the B piece. Slash along the curve, cutting to, but not through, the stitching.

Arrange the cut pieces in front of you, according to Fig. 143 to form 16 squares. As you join the pieces following directions below, return them to their positions to be sure the pattern develops properly.

Here's the rule we use for joining curved pieces: Pin on the concave side and sew on the convex. Carefully pin an A to a B along the curved pencil lines (Fig. 145). Work with the concave side A up and stretch it as you pin.

Then turn the fabric over and stitch on the convex side. You may want to baste first, then machine-stitch, or you may decide to sew the seam completely by hand. When you finish, the stay-stitching should not show. Trim and finger-press the completed seam.

Join all the curved seams to form 15 more squares for the Drunkard's Path.

Finishing the block

Line up the 16 squares according to Fig. 143. Sew four small squares together to form the top row. Join the squares to form the remaining three rows. Finally, sew the rows together to complete the block.

We hope that the old superstition connected with this pattern did not affect you as you worked.

GRANDMOTHER'S FAN

The traditional quilt block shown in Fig. 146 combines curved piecing and appliqué.

Young ladies of the colonial period were taught the proper use of the fan, so it was natural for the fan to find its way into a quilt design. Grandmother's Fan is perfect for a sampler quilt because you can use most of your fabrics in the block.

The solid colors of the foundation square and corner piece also provide spaces for some extra quilting, and we offer three rose patterns (page 104) for this. Bias binding can be used to finish the outside edge of the fan.

You will need three templates. First, find the 15"-square template you made in Chapter 3, or draft a new one. Then make templates from curved patterns A and B on page 103.

On the *wrong* side of the fabric, trace and cut (adding ½" seam allowances):

A—8 of assorted colors and prints
B—1 of solid color No. 1
15" square—1 of solid color No. 2

Place the fan spokes A in front of you and piece them together as you did the Dresden Plate in Chapter 5. Then join the pieced A fan to the B corner piece. Here you are faced with concave and convex curves again. Staystitch, pin-baste and sew the curves together, just as you did the curves in Drunkard's Path (see "Joining the curves" on page 97).

Place the completed fan on the foundation square and pin in place. Baste the raw edges of the outside curve in place, then cover it with a strip of bias tape in a contrasting color. Attach the tape with the appliqué stitch. (An alternate method of finishing this outside curved edge is to turn under the seam allowance and attach to the foundation

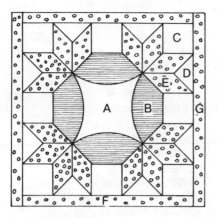

Fig. 147   Hands All Around
(See also plate 15)

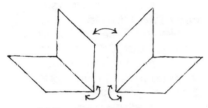

Fig. 148   Joining the diamonds

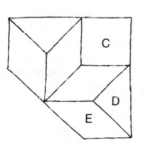

Fig. 149   Forming a corner

Fig. 150   Piecing the block

with the appliqué stitch.)

Finally, draw the rose quilting designs on the plain area in a way that is pleasing to your eye. (Refer to "Extra quilting lines," on page 61.)

If you wonder about quilting through the double thickness on some areas of this block, just cut away the foundation fabric where it is covered by appliqué.

HANDS ALL AROUND

A popular square dance was the inspiration for the old quilt pattern shown in Fig. 147. This probably is the most difficult pattern in the book because it combines curved piecing, diamonds, and a narrow border or sashing.

Don't panic. You have used all the techniques required for this block. This pattern just puts them all together.

Hands All Around is ideal for your signature block. That nice A piece in the center can be embroidered with your name and the date to set you apart as a quilter of distinction.

Make the five templates from patterns on page 105, then draft two rectangles—7⁄8x13¼" (F) and 7⁄8x15" (G)—for the outside border. Choose three fabrics—two solid colors, one light and one dark, plus one print.

On the *wrong* side of the fabric, trace and cut (adding ½" seam allowances):

A—1 of solid color No. 1
B—4 of solid color No. 2
C—8 of solid color No. 1
D—8 of solid color No. 1
E—16 of print
F—2 of print
G—2 of print

Arrange the pieces in front of you, following Fig. 147.

Work with one corner section at a time. Sew diamonds E together in pairs, then join the pairs (Fig. 148). Sew only on the pencil lines. All stitches that stray into the seam allowance must be removed.

Next, piece in square C and two D triangles (Fig. 149). Repeat this process to complete the three other corners.

For the center section (Fig. 150), sew the four B pieces to the center A with curved piecing, as in Drunkard's Path (see "Joining the curves" on page 97). Then add squares C to the B pieces.

Finally, add the corner units. First sew a unit to the center B piece, then join along the C pieces.

There! Wasn't this block worth all the effort?

PAPER WORK APPLIQUÉ

You were introduced to paper work when you made Grandmother's Flower Garden in Chapter 5. Here are two more designs—one with diamonds and one with curves—that depend on paper templates to keep the shapes exact.

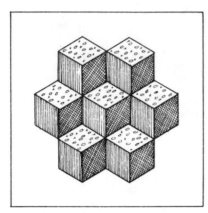

Fig. 151   Baby Blocks
(See also plate 15)

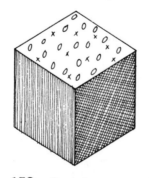

Fig. 152   Forming one cube

BABY BLOCKS

This design, also called Tumbling Blocks, is a challenge in diamonds (Fig. 151). These diamonds are special because they are sewed together in threes to form cubes. They are called regular diamonds, while those used to make the Eight-Pointed Star are called long diamonds and do not form cubes.

Choose four fabrics—two solid colors and one print for the blocks, and a third solid color for the foundation block. We used the same arrangement of fabric pieces for each three-diamond cube. However, it is possible to use a mix of fabrics as long as you repeat one color in the same position on each cube. This is necessary to maintain the optical illusion that the design creates.

The beauty of this quilt block depends on precise workmanship, and you achieve this by cutting paper patterns drawn to exact size.

First, make a template from the pattern on page 106. Then trace the template on paper 21 times and cut (without adding seam allowances).

To cut the fabric, position a paper diamond on the *wrong* side of the fabric and pin in place. (Refer to "Two ways to cut diamonds", page 86.) Cut (adding ½" seam allowances):

    7 of solid color No. 1
    7 of solid color No. 2
    7 of print

Find your 15"-square template and use it to trace and cut (adding ½" seam allowances) one foundation square of solid color No. 3.

Work with the individual diamonds. Turn the seam allowances over the sides of paper on each diamond and baste in place. Don't worry about the excess fabric at the points. These seam allowances will be hidden as the cubes are formed.

Take three diamonds, each a different fabric, and whip them together to form one small cube, as in Fig. 152. (See whipping stitch on page 50.) Repeat the process to complete six more identical cubes.

Sew the cubes together, following Fig. 151. Trim the seam allowances to 1/8". Press the appliqué, remove the bastings and pop the papers (refer to "Popping the papers", page 50).

Center the design on the foundation block and baste. Appliqué it in place, then remove the bastings.

Isn't it fun to watch the optical illusion develop? Good workmanship is its own reward.

Fig. 153 Clamshell
(See also plate 15)

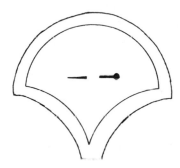

Fig. 154 Using template to cut fabric

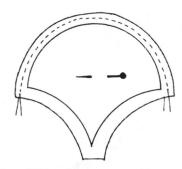

Fig. 155 Gathering thread along curve

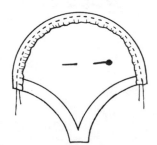

Fig. 156 Shaping fabric over curve

CLAMSHELL

The second advanced block in paper work is called Clamshell (Fig. 153), and this design lets you use a variety of fabrics. (We used eight different ones in our sample block.) Like Grandmother's Fan, Clamshell offers continuity by repeating many of the colors and prints in your quilt.

You can arrange the shells in a random manner as we did, or follow a planned order so that certain prints or colors run in a diagonal line.

First, use your 15"-square template to trace a foundation square of muslin. Cut out the fabric, adding a ½" seam allowance on all sides.

The technique for Clamshell is different from the one used in Baby Blocks. Instead of making a separate template for each shell, you'll need to cut only four or five templates; each one may be used many times. Make the templates from something like tagboard (file folder material) so that they are thin enough to pin to fabric, but sturdy enough to be used over and over. The pattern is on page 106.

It takes 36 Clamshells to cover the block, and success with this design depends on shells with nice, smooth tops. To achieve this, we suggest you follow these steps for each shell:

1. Place a template on the *wrong* side of the fabric and pin (Fig. 154). Cut around the template, adding a ½" seam allowance.

2. With the template still attached, machine- or hand-stitch a gathering thread along the top curve, at least ¼" outside the template (Fig. 155). (If you use the machine, let the presser foot ride along the edge of the template as a guide. Loosen the tension a bit and use a long stitch).

3. Pull the thread (the bobbin thread if you are machine-stitching) to gather the fabric. Fit the seam allowance over the template (Fig. 156). Work with the fabric until it is firm and smooth along the top curve (no wrinkles). Press well.

4. Unpin the template and position it on the right side of the fabric shell, keeping the top curves even. Holding the template in place, use a No. 5H or 6H pencil to trace along the lower curves, marking the fabric.

To assemble the block, place the foundation square on a table, with the pencil markings for seam allowances facing up. Position a row of shells at the top of the foundation square, with the tops of the shells just meeting the seam allowance (Fig. 157). Pin the shells in place. To make the block appear to be completely covered with shells, tuck bits of extra fabric between the shells along the top edge.

Baste the shells in place. Then use the appliqué stitch (Fig. 56) to attach the top curves to the foundation fabric. These stitches will also catch the extra fabric along the top edge.

Add a second row of

Fig. 157 Appliqueing shells to foundation

shells, fitting the tops along the penciled curves on the first row of shells. You will need five shells for this row. Let the end pieces extend beyond the block. Baste and appliqué in place.

Keep adding rows, alternating with four and five shells, until the block is covered.

Finally, turn the block over and trim off excess fabric that extends beyond the block. Remove all bastings.

There! You have finished the last quilt block in the book.

CONGRATULATIONS!

If you have pieced and appliquéd all the blocks we suggested, you have mastered 37 different designs. We hope that, along the way, you have encouraged your husband, sons, daughters or friends to join you in the venture. (We find that husbands can be a big help in measuring patterns, choosing fabrics or even working blocks, especially when an exhibit deadline is near.)

We know that you have had some tense moments trying to get triangles to fit properly and pattern pieces to go into the right place. Quilting requires patience, concentration and much "stick-to-itiveness."

We hope that your experience has been fun and challenging and that this book will guide you through years of quilting adventures.

Happy quilting and God Bless,
—Love,

Jessie & Marian

Patterns

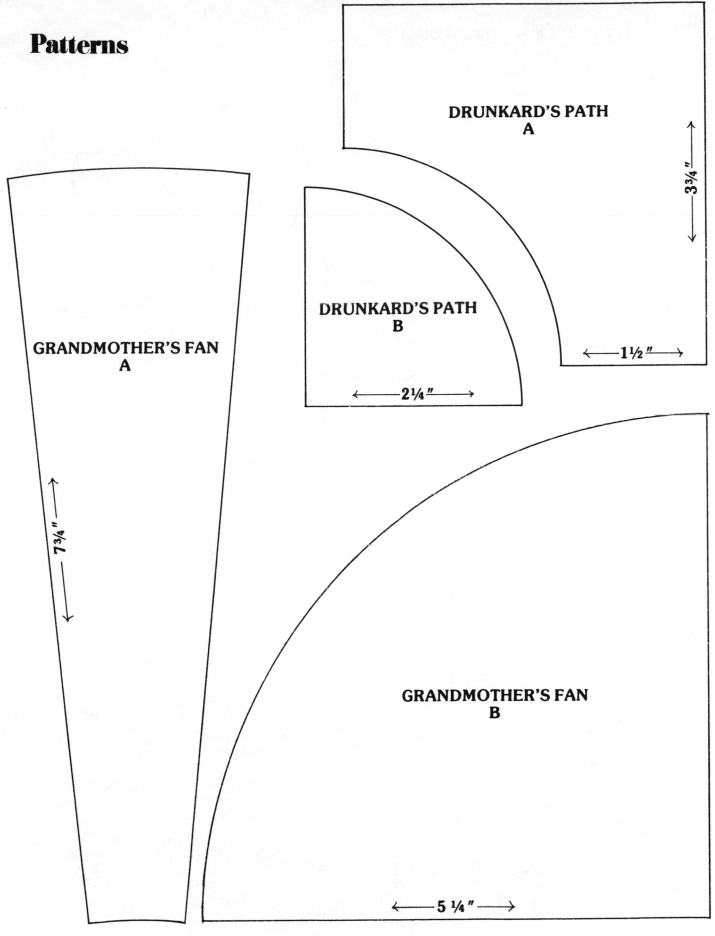

DRUNKARD'S PATH
A

3¾"

DRUNKARD'S PATH
B

1½"

2¼"

GRANDMOTHER'S FAN
A

7¾"

GRANDMOTHER'S FAN
B

5 ¼"

Quilting designs for GRANDMOTHER'S FAN

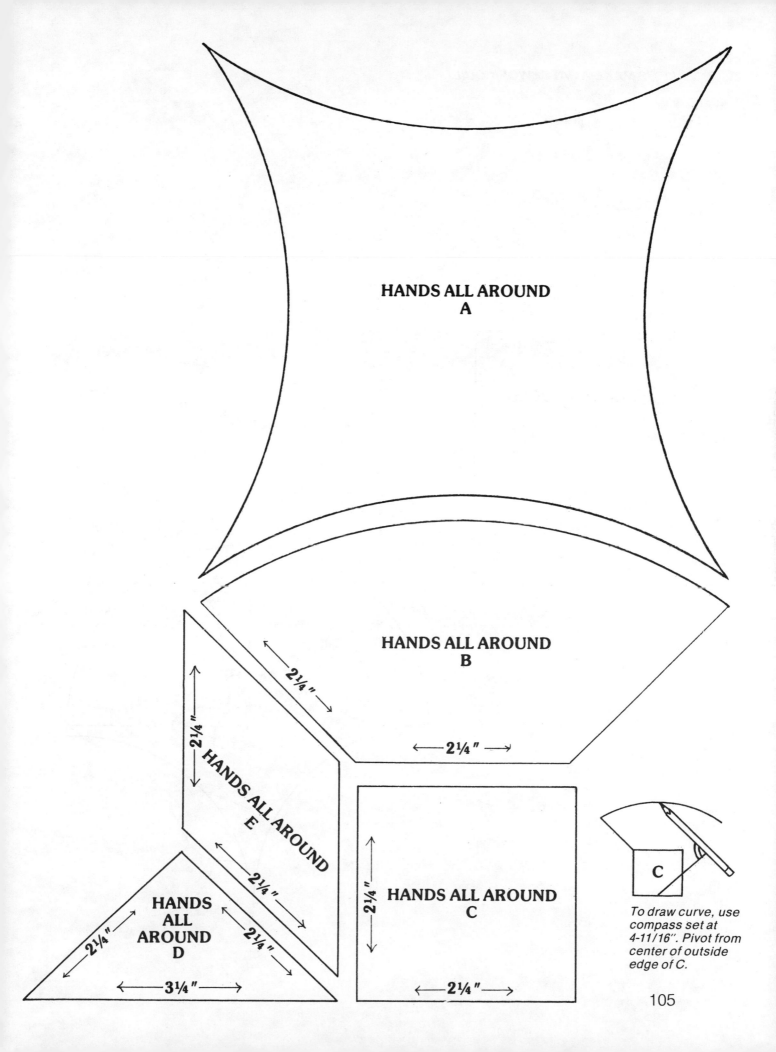

HANDS ALL AROUND
A

HANDS ALL AROUND
B

2¼"

2¼"

2¼"

HANDS ALL AROUND
E

2¼"

2¼"

HANDS
ALL
AROUND
D

2¼"

2¼"

3¼"

2¼"

HANDS ALL AROUND
C

2¼"

2¼"

C

To draw curve, use compass set at 4-11/16". Pivot from center of outside edge of C.

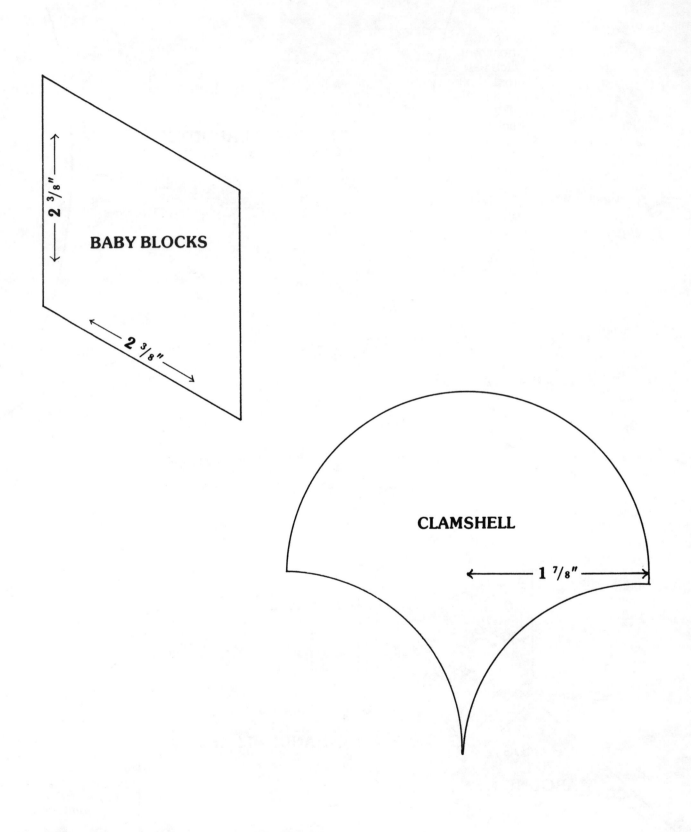

BABY BLOCKS

2 ³/₈"

2 ³/₈"

CLAMSHELL

1 ⁷/₈"

Reminders

1. Be accurate when you draft templates.

2. Trace pattern templates for pieced work on the wrong side of the fabric. Trace pattern templates for most appliqué work on the right side of the fabric.

3. Place edges of squares and rectangles on the straight grain. Place the longest side of a triangle on the straight grain.

Place a diamond so that two edges are on the straight grain, or so the widest part of the diamond runs along the straight grain.

Place a free-form shape for appliqué so the center of the design runs along the straight grain.

4. Sharpen your pencil frequently when you are tracing templates on fabric.

5. Add ½" seam allowances when you cut out fabric pieces and blocks. Trim them to just under ¼" (to ¹/₈" for diamonds) after each seam is stitched.

6. Arrange all pieces of a quilt block, right side up, to form the design, then begin to sew them together.

7. Follow these basic steps: trace, cut, pin-baste, stitch, trim, finger-press.

8. Prepare for quilting by basting the layers together. Always baste from the center outward.

9. Always quilt from the center outward.

Extra quilting designs

Extra quilting designs

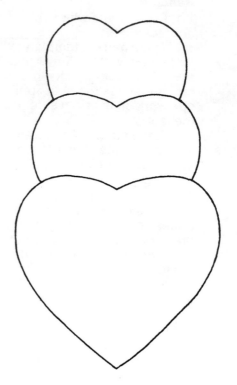

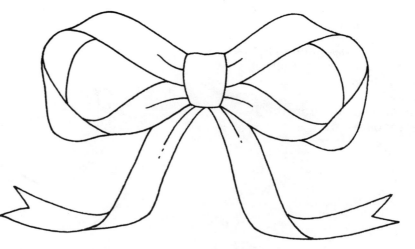

Index